A SACRED VOICE
IS CALLING

A SACRED VOICE IS CALLING

Personal Vocation and Social Conscience

John Neafsey

ORBIS BOOKS

Maryknoll, New York 10545

Founded in 1970, Orbis Books endeavors to publish works that enlighten the mind, nourish the spirit, and challenge the conscience. The publishing arm of the Maryknoll Fathers and Brothers, Orbis seeks to explore the global dimensions of the Christian faith and mission, to invite dialogue with diverse cultures and religious traditions, and to serve the cause of reconciliation and peace. The books published reflect the views of their authors and do not represent the official position of the Maryknoll Society. To learn more about Maryknoll and Orbis Books, please visit our website at www.maryknoll.org.

Library of Congress Cataloging-in-Publication Data

Neafsey, John.
    A sacred voice is calling : personal vocation and social conscience /
John Neafsey.
        p. cm.
    Includes index.
    ISBN-13: 978-1-57075-645-0
    1. Vocation—Catholic Church. 2. Christian sociology—Catholic
Church. I. Title.
    BX1795.W67N43 2006
    248.4—dc22
                                        2005026998

To
Maura, Bryan, and Rosie

Perhaps a new spirit is rising among us.
If it is, let us trace its movements well and pray
that our own inner being may be sensitive to its guidance,
for we are deeply in need of a new way beyond the darkness
that seems so close all around us.

—Martin Luther King Jr.

CONTENTS

PREFACE

Tell me, what is it you plan to do with your one wild and precious life?
—Mary Oliver, "The Summer Day"[1]

FOR AS LONG AS I CAN REMEMBER, I have been pre-occupied with questions about vocation. What does it mean to find and follow a personal calling? How do we know what we are meant to do with our precious time and talents and treasure during our short lives here on this earth? How, ex-actly, do we "hear" calls anyway? What happens if we miss our calling—maybe because we fail to hear it or don't have the courage to follow it? Is there any reliable way to tell the dif-ference between the "still, small voice" of our authentic calling and all of the other distracting, competing, counterfeit voices in our culture and in ourselves that tend to get us on the wrong track?

These are big questions, and a lot is riding on the depth and generosity and courage of our answers to them. Ulti-mately, such questions are answered not with words, but with choices we make about how to live our lives. When we are wrestling with our callings in important matters of love or work or conscience, it sometimes feels as if our very souls are at stake. They are! I mean this not just in the sense that deci-sions made during our earthly lifetime affect our prospects for salvation in the world to come, but in terms of the pre-cious opportunity we are given to save our integrity and dig-nity and humanity in *this* life by discovering who we are, what we have to offer, where we stand, and how we can help.[2] My hope is that this book will be of some assistance to readers who are engaged in this high-stakes process of personal discernment and self-discovery.

As a person who works both as a practicing clinical psychologist and as a college theology teacher, I have an interdisciplinary interest in the psychology and spirituality of vocation, especially in the ways these come together in the affective or heart dimension of our human experience. Vocation is very much a matter of the heart. In both my teaching and my clinical work, I am often in the privileged position of helping people learn to listen to their hearts for clues about which life directions hold the promise and potential for greater emotional and spiritual health. Calls come to us, first of all, by way of the heart, and careful attention to the movements and inclinations of our hearts is one of the primary tools we have for hearing the "inner voice" that calls us to our destiny.

Calls also inevitably require us to undergo a *change* of heart through a sometimes painful—but always redemptive—process of personal conversion and transformation. It is not easy to let go of old ways of thinking and feeling and acting, but we are nonetheless invited to become *new persons*. "I will give them one heart, and put a new spirit within them," says the prophet Ezekiel. "I will remove the heart of stone from their flesh and give them a heart of flesh."[3] The "heart of flesh" of which Ezekiel speaks is an open heart, a compassionate heart, a heart capable of being moved by need and suffering and of moving *us* to an appropriately human response. The way I will be using the term *social conscience* is grounded in this rich biblical notion of the heart.

In recent years, especially since the 9/11 tragedy and the onset of the Iraq War, I have found myself increasingly preoccupied with the moral, social, and political dimensions of vocation. I am especially interested in the role of social conscience in callings to compassionate service and responsible global citizenship. This includes the stirrings of ethical passion that incline some people of conscience to engage in principled opposition and resistance to various forms of social injustice and inhumanity, of which there is no shortage in our world. In this sense, vocation can be understood as the call of conscience, or as a call *to* conscience.[4] In a global situation of expanding injustice and inequality, and in a nation caught up in a war regarded as unwise and unjust by most of the world, it seems to me that an uneasy conscience may be one of the best places to listen for the whisper of the Spirit that calls us to a better way.

The book is guided by a broad, interdisciplinary, ecumenical view of vocation. Although I stand in the Roman Catholic tradition, my understanding of vocation is based on the assumption that the intuition of a sacred purpose for our lives is a universal or archetypal human phenomenon. In other words, *everyone* has a vocation. This includes Catholics and Protestants, Christians and non-Christians, religious and non-religious people, those who use "God-talk" and those who don't. For many, referring to God (by whatever name) is the only way to adequately express the profound sense of depth and sacredness they feel in connection with their life's work or purpose. Others, less comfortable or familiar with religious language for various reasons, prefer to describe their callings in non-religious terms. Ultimately, the words we use are less important than the integrity and heart with which we pursue our callings.

The title of this book comes from a song heard in a childhood vision of Black Elk, the great Native American visionary and healer: "Behold, a sacred voice is calling you; all over the sky a sacred voice is calling."[5] Rich examples from Black Elk's remarkable vocation story can be found throughout the book.

I am grateful to Daniel Hernández–Salazar, the award-winning photographer from Guatemala, for permission to use his striking photograph on the cover. Titled "Para Que Todos Lo Sepan" ("So That All Shall Know"), the photo of the indigenous angel was originally used for the cover of a 1998 human rights report that resulted from a unique pastoral initiative carried out by the Catholic Church in Guatemala. Known as the "Recovery of Historical Memory" project (better known by its initials as REMHI),[6] the initiative involved the careful and sensitive collection and documentation of thousands of personal testimonies from victims and witnesses of human rights violations (mostly impoverished Mayan people from the highlands of the country) during Guatemala's horrifically cruel civil war. Bishop Juan Gerardi, the coordinator of the Human Rights Office of the Archdiocese of Guatemala, presided over the project. Two days after the REMHI report was publicly released at a ceremony marking the occasion at the Metropolitan Cathedral in Guatemala City on April 24, 1998, Gerardi was murdered by a team of military assassins to punish and silence him for his efforts to make sure "that all should know" about what had happened to his people. More about Bishop Gerardi and REHMI can be found in chapter 4. Among other projects, Daniel Hernández–Salazar has been involved in photographing human remains exhumed from hundreds of mass graves of massacre victims around the country. The wings of the "Para Que Todos Lo Sepan" angel are human bones.

I am especially grateful to the Lilly Endowment's Programs for the Theological Exploration of Vocation (PTEV) project for a grant to support the writing of the book. Since 1999, eighty-eight U.S. colleges and universities have received generous PTEV grants to establish or strengthen programs aimed to help students, faculty, and staff discern and follow their individual and collective callings. Kim Maphis Early, the national program coordinator, is a gem. Her gracious and skilled work with the diverse collection of PTEV-supported schools is a true ministry. Appreciation also goes to Lucien Roy and Fr. John Haughey, who have played key roles in nurturing the local incarnation of this vocation initiative, the EVOKE program at Loyola University Chicago.

Robert Ellsberg, editor-in-chief of Orbis Books, has been consistently enthusiastic about the book from the very beginning. It has been an honor and a pleasure to work with him and the staff at Orbis. Special thanks also to my brother, Jim Neafsey, for his careful reading and critique of drafts of the book and for his brotherly love and mentoring for as long as I can remember. I'm ever grateful to my parents, Ed and Louise Neafsey, for their loving support for "Operation Book."

It is hard to find words to express my gratitude to Maura, my loving wife. The poet Yeats says it better than I ever could:

> Wine comes in at the mouth
> And love comes in at the eye;
> That's all we shall know for truth
> Before we grow old and die.
> I lift the glass to my mouth,
> I look at you, and I sigh.[7]

Finally, I am blessed beyond words every day by my children, Bryan and Rosie. When I forget, they help me remember that love is what true callings are all about.

1

INTRODUCTION
Personal Vocation and Social Conscience

The place God calls you to is the place where your deep gladness and the world's deep hunger meet.
    —Frederick Buechner[1]

For me the Voice of God, of Conscience, of Truth, or the Inner Voice or "the Still Small Voice" mean one and the same thing.
    —Gandhi[2]

VOCATION is not only about "me" and my personal fulfillment, but about "us" and the common good. In Buechner's words, our callings are found in the places where our "deep gladness" and the "world's deep hunger" meet, on the holy ground where our heart's desire comes together with what the world most needs *from* us. Authentic vocational discernment, therefore, seeks a proper balance between inward listening *to* our hearts and outward, socially engaged listening *with* our hearts to the realities of the world in which we live. These come together in our heart's response to the needs and sufferings of the world. "What matters," writes José Garcia, "is that the world should touch the heart and that the heart should go out towards the world."[3]

In this chapter I will sketch out a broad, interdisciplinary, ecumenical view of vocation as a foundation for the book. Along the way, I will explore a number of key psychological and spiritual dimensions of the inner voice that are relevant to vocational discernment. Social conscience will be understood as an essential component of this sacred voice that calls us to both personal authenticity and social responsibility.

MEANINGS OF VOCATION

The word *vocation* has different meanings and associations for different people. When I talk to classes or groups of people about vocation, the first thing I do is ask the question: "What comes to mind when you hear the word *vocation?*"

People commonly associate vocation either with the call to ordained ministry or vowed religious life or with the popular secular understanding of vocation as being synonymous with a job, occupation, or career. These are valid, but incomplete, understandings of vocation. Some people do have special callings to priesthood or ministry or religious life, but most don't. This does not mean that these others don't have a vocation, but rather that God has another purpose in mind for them, something else for them to do or be. Similarly, though the kind of work we do is an important dimension of our calling, it is important not to define the rich, complex phenomenon of vocation too narrowly or exclusively in terms of job or profession.

Although finding meaningful work that matches our God-given interests and talents is an important component of vocational discernment, there is more to life than work, and vocation is much bigger than what we do to earn a living. American obsessions with productivity, career achievement, and upward mobility are hazardous to our emotional, spiritual, and moral health. "The trouble with the rat race," goes the saying, "is that even if you win, you're still a rat." In my experience, the task of vocational discernment for driven, overworked, and harried people (a category that often includes myself) requires stepping back from and taking a critical look at the particular ways in which our lives are out of balance. Sometimes careful listening reveals that our true calling is not to more work, or better work, or different work, but to a reordering of our priorities and a more balanced life.

Vocation potentially touches and encompasses *every* level and dimension of our lives. This includes our family life, our love life, our creative interests and pursuits, and our politics. Basically, *anything* we do with our time and talents and resources can be infused with a sense of vocation. Callings can also be experienced in relation to any or all of the multiple roles in which we find ourselves at any given time (e.g., friend, parent, daughter, son, sibling, spouse, partner, parishioner, co-worker, neighbor, citizen, etc.).

Callings in different areas or dimensions of our lives are often interrelated in complex and mysterious ways. For example, I experienced a profound sense of vocation when I fell in love with my wife and recognized that she was the one with whom I was meant to spend my life. We both wanted to have children, which we interpreted as a mutual calling to share the joys and responsibilities of parenthood together. As it turned out, our particular path to parenthood was through the process of international adoption—itself a kind of calling. We eventually adopted two wonderful children from Guatemala.

As we have come to know and love our little son and daughter, we have also come to know and love their homeland in ways we never could have imagined. The heart connection to our children has opened us up to the heartbreak and desperation and traumatic history of their beautiful country. We find ourselves in an ongoing process of discerning our responsibilities as privileged North Americans in relation to our Latin American neighbors to the south, who are now, in a very real sense, *family* to us. Among other things, this has prompted me to volunteer my services as a psychologist at a local program that serves survivors of torture from Central America and other areas of the world. And so, in these matters of the heart, one calling often seems to lead to another.

It is also possible to experience different callings at different times of our lives, or to experience multiple callings at any particular time of our life. Our dream of what a meaningful life looks like at age twenty may look very different at age forty. Persons approaching retirement are challenged to think of vocation in new ways as they contemplate what to do with their time and talents after their formal professional career is finished. A person whose identity has been primarily tied to work and career may feel a need to re-evaluate his or her priorities in the context of the competing demands and callings of family and parenting at a different stage of life.

Although some vocational decisions center around lifetime commitments in love or work that affect the fundamental direction of our lives, callings also come to us in response to very specific challenges or issues that present themselves at particular times of our individual or collective lives. For example, we may be called to find creative and courageous ways to cope with a personal emotional crisis, a death or serious illness in the family, the loss of a job, a personal addiction, caring for a child with special needs, or any other life situation that presents us with an opportunity for emotional or spiritual growth.

Circumstances in the life of our local or national or global communities can also call upon us to rise to the occasion, to take a stand, to take a risk, to do the right thing. On a local level, concerned parents might experience a calling to come together to figure out how to assertively respond to gang activity that is making the neighborhood playground unhealthy and unsafe for their children. On a national or global level, individual citizens or churches might experience callings to discern their individual or collective response to the Iraq War, torture, capital punishment, poverty, abortion, racism, sexism, or any other important moral issue of our time.

It is also important to keep in mind that vocation is not only about what we *do* but about *who we are*. Evelyn and James Whitehead put it this way: "Vocation is a gradual revelation—of me to myself by God.... It is who we are, trying to happen."[4] Our callings have to do with the *kind* of person we are called to be, the quality of our personhood, the values and attitudes we embody, the integrity and authenticity of our lives. From this vantage point, vocation is less about the particular things we do and more about the spirit with which we do them. "Character is not what you do," writes James Hillman, "it's the way you do it."[5]

"What does the LORD require of you," asks the prophet Micah, "but to do justice, and to love kindness, and to walk humbly with your God?"[6] Whether we are a doctor or a minister, an artist or a taxi driver, a nanny or a teacher, our fundamental human vocation is to become just, loving, and humble persons during our short lives here on this earth. Conducting ourselves with justice, love, and humility always begins with how we treat our loved ones and the people in the circle of our everyday lives. As we consider our social responsibilities as citizens of our country and our world, though, our callings extend beyond our personal circle to an ever-expanding network of connection and solidarity with people both far and near.

THE VOICE

The Latin roots of the word *vocation* (*vocare*, "to call" and *vox*, "voice") center around the experience of hearing a call or voice. "The original meaning of 'to have a vocation,'" wrote

Carl Jung, "is 'to be addressed by a voice.'"[7] But *who,* or *what,* is calling?

From a spiritual perspective, of course, *God* is the Caller. The voice of vocation is the Voice of God. A divine source of wisdom, mysteriously both beyond and within ourselves, guides us in the path of our true calling and summons us to our destiny. Thomas Kelly, writing from the Quaker tradition, says it beautifully:

> Deep within us all, there is an amazing inner sanctuary of the soul, a holy place, a Divine Center, a speaking Voice, to which we may continuously return. Eternity is at our hearts, pressing upon our time-torn lives, warming us with intimations of an astounding destiny, calling us home unto itself.[8]

There are other ways to understand the Voice. From a psychological perspective, callings can be seen as originating in our deepest and most authentic self, our "true self." A popular self-help book calls it our "best self": "Listening to the call of your natural vocation requires the capacity to hear the voice of your own best self and the capacity to respond effectively to it."[9] Jung named this deep center of authenticity the "Self," even going so far as to capitalize the first letter of the word to distinguish it from our everyday ego identity and to highlight its association with things deep and sacred.[10]

Jung, an unconventional psychological theorist with a deep interest in spiritual matters, understood the sense of vocation as an urge to self-realization originating in the deep, unconscious, inner self of the human person. From his perspective, the voice of vocation is the voice of our inmost self or conscience, which, for him, was the psychological equivalent of God.[11] The Self functions like an inner voice that calls and guides us through a life-long process of self-discovery and self-realization that Jung called *individuation.* This process of becoming ourselves requires an ever-growing consciousness of the unfolding truth of who we are, along with ongoing efforts to live our lives in accord with it. According to Edward Whitmont, the Self "... generates the individuation drive, the urge to become what we are, as well as the genuine individual conscience, which, in its psychological significance, is likened to *vox Dei*, the 'voice of God.'"[12]

The notion of an essential inner self calling for recognition and expression has a rich history in Christianity and diverse other spiritual traditions of the world. Thomas Merton writes:

> In Sufism, Zen Buddhism and in many other religious or spiritual traditions, emphasis is placed on the call to fulfill certain obscure yet urgent potentialities in the ground of one's being, to "become someone" that one already (potentially) is, the person one is truly meant to be. Zen calls this awakening a recognition of "your original face before you were born."[13]

Conscience is another expression of the Voice encountered across diverse cultures and spiritual traditions, and it also bridges the disciplines of theology and psychology. In the popular imagination, conscience is associated with the "little voice in our heads" that helps us recognize the difference between right and wrong. It is helpful to make a distinction between *personal* and *social* conscience. Although both are dimensions of the same inner voice, the former can be seen as applying primarily to matters of private, personal morality, while the latter is more concerned with public morality and the common good.

Theologically, it can be said that God *uses* the inclinations of our true self, the promptings of conscience, to help and guide and call us through decisions big and small toward the goal or purpose for which we were created. According to

Russell Connors and Patrick McCormick, the ultimate goal is an ever-deeper and fuller sense of humanity that can be likened to *sainthood*:

> In that most secret core of our being we are haunted by a moral siren summoning us to become more and more fully human, to transform ourselves into increasingly loving and principled adults, indeed, to become saints.[14]

A striking example of a Voice experience is found in the life of Gandhi, a man widely regarded as one of the most saintly, loving, principled persons of modern times. At the time, he was jailed in India's Yeravda Central Prison on charges related to his nonviolent resistance to the oppression of the "untouchables" (the destitute underclass in India) by unjust attitudes and policies rooted in Hindu tradition and Indian society. On the night of April 28, 1933, Gandhi had the following experience:

> One experience stands quite distinctly in my memory. It relates to my twenty-one days' fast for the removal of untouchability. At about twelve o'clock in the night something wakes me up suddenly and some voice—within me or without, I cannot say— whispers, "Thou must go on fast." "How many days?" I ask. "Twenty-one days." "When does it begin?" I ask. "You begin tomorrow." I went quietly off to sleep after making the decision. I did not tell anything to my companions until after the morning prayer. I placed into their hands a slip of paper announcing my decision and asking them not to argue with me as the decision was irrevocable. Well, the doctors thought that I would not survive the fast. But

something within me said I would and that I must go forward. That kind of experience has never in my life happened before or after that date.

The first question that has puzzled many is about the voice of God. What was it? What did I hear? Was there any person I saw? If not, how was the voice conveyed to me? These are pertinent questions.

I saw no form. I have never tried for it, for I have always believed God to be without form. But what I did hear was like a voice from afar and yet quite near. It was as unmistakable as some human voice, definitely speaking to me, and irresistible. I was not dreaming at the time I heard the voice. The hearing of the voice was preceded by a terrific struggle within me. Suddenly the voice came upon me. I listened, made certain it was the voice and the struggle ceased. I was calm. The determination was made accordingly, the date and hour of the fast fixed. Joy came over me. . . . I felt refreshed.

Could I give any further evidence that it was truly the voice I heard and that it was not an echo of my own heated imagination? I have no further evidence to convince the skeptic. He [or she] is free to say it was all self-delusion. It may well have been so. I can offer no proof to the contrary. But I can say this: that the unanimous verdict of the whole world against me could not shake me from my belief that what I heard was the true Voice of God.[15]

Gandhi's formidable intellect and familiarity with skeptical modern views of such experiences make his account all the more compelling. Freud, for example, would likely have reduced Gandhi's voice experience to a form of wishful thinking or fantasy. In modern psychiatry, the experience might suggest a worrisome loss of contact with "reality" and be labeled an "auditory hallucination."

Gandhi himself, however, was quite sure that he was not confused or out of touch with reality. Rather, he was convinced that he had actually been *in touch* with a deeper, intangible, mysterious dimension of reality that is of an order different from our usual categories of rational thinking and perception. About such experiences, William James wrote: "There is in the human consciousness a sense of reality, a feeling of objective presence, a perception of what we may call 'something there,' more deep and more general than any of the special and particular senses by which the current psychology supposes existent realities to be originally revealed."[16]

Most of us, of course, are not blessed with the depth of experience or unshakable sense of certitude and clarity of great-souled people like Gandhi. This does not mean, however, that the Voice does not speak to average human beings. It just means we need to listen for it more carefully.

LEARNING TO LISTEN

The saints, mystics, shamans, and prophets in our midst are gifted with unusual capacities for hearing and perception. Most of the rest of us, though, can probably recognize ourselves in the category of people Jesus diagnosed as "hard of hearing":

> With them indeed is fulfilled the prophecy of Isaiah that says: "You will indeed listen, but never understand, and you will indeed look, but never perceive. For this people's heart has grown dull, and their ears are hard of hearing, and they have shut their eyes; so that they might not look with their eyes, and listen

with their ears, and understand with their heart and turn—and I would heal them."[17]

It takes practice and hard work to develop "eyes to see" and "ears to hear." To do so, we must commit ourselves to cultivating the art and skill of what William Least Heat Moon has called "the god-awful difficulty of just paying attention."[18] It is not easy to overcome our inclinations toward dullness and numbness and complacency, to cultivate a heart that is open and responsive to calls when they come to us. Saint Ignatius Loyola likened this process of learning new ways of seeing and hearing and feeling to an education or "schooling" of the heart.[19]

To make any progress at all in this kind of education, we must possess an appropriate sense of humility, which is only fitting for those who have a lot to learn. In the Zen Buddhist tradition, the recommended attitude is referred to as "beginner's mind."[20] In the words of Isaiah, we must learn to "listen as those who are taught":

> Morning by morning he wakens—
> wakens my ear
> to listen as those who are taught.
> The Lord God has opened my ear.[21]

Time-honored spiritual practices of prayer and meditation can be seen as techniques for developing our listening skills so that we are able to listen more consciously and intentionally for the inner voice of the Spirit. On a psychological level, prayer is a way of focusing attention on our inner experience so as to establish a dialogue or connection with our inner self, to listen for messages that come to us from within. A parallel between prayer and the dialogue with the inner self is found in the diary of Etty Hillesum, a deeply spiritual young Jewish woman from the Netherlands who was sent to the death camps by the Nazis during the Holocaust: "When I pray," Etty wrote, "I hold a silly, naïve, or deadly serious dialogue with what is deepest inside me, which for the sake of convenience I call God."[22]

The Voice, however, does not speak only from within ourselves; it calls to us through other human beings, and so we must also learn to listen carefully and respectfully to what other people have to say. Eduardo Galeano captures the inherent sacredness and dignity and value of the *human voice*:

> When it is genuine, when it is born of the need to speak, no one can stop the human voice. When denied a mouth, it speaks with the hands or the eyes, or the pores, or anything at all. Because every single one of us has something to say to the others, something that deserves to be celebrated or forgiven by others.[23]

"Perhaps the single most important skill that should be taught to all persons," says Wilson Van Dusen, "is the capacity to really see, hear, and understand others. Such a skill is useful in dealing with everyone—friends, relatives, strangers."[24] The capacity to really listen, to put aside our own concerns for the moment, to feel or imagine ourselves in the world of another person and then to communicate our empathic understanding to that person in such a way that he or she feels *heard* or *understood* is the foundation for all genuine relationship and solidarity between human beings. It is also the primary ingredient in the healing process of psychotherapy, which has been called the "talking cure." Learning to listen well to other people is itself a kind of spiritual practice or discipline.

Finally, and most pertinent to the issue of social conscience, listening to others is the first step in any authentic commitment to social justice. Dan Hartnett, an American Jesuit who lived and worked among the poor in the slums of Lima, Peru, for twenty-three years, says such commitments can grow only out of direct personal contact with suffering people and the distressing social realities in which they live. We start by listening to the personal stories and experiences of the poor:

> In the area of justice, the turn to experience has a specific meaning. It suggests that a commitment to justice does not begin with abstract concepts, as important as these may be, but with attention to concrete experiences of social suffering. In other words, we take the first step in the direction of justice by intentionally shifting our attention from ourselves and by focusing on the daily experiences of those who suffer injustice.... It begins with the effort to put ourselves in the shoes of the other, especially those in extreme poverty or who are enduring painful forms of social exclusion.... A true concern for justice never begins with definitions but with real faces of injustice.... Without this kind of direct contact with everyday suffering, without sustained attention to real histories of pain, justice will never become something a person truly cares about, something that constitutes a real priority, something to which one is willing to make a commitment.[25]

LEARNING TO LIVE

Listening carefully helps us learn how to live in this world. It helps us cultivate the kind of emotional, spiritual, and moral intelligence we need to make life choices that are suited to who we are and who we are called to become. In an essay entitled "Learning to Live," Thomas Merton writes:

> Life consists in learning to live on one's own, sponta-
> neous, freewheeling: to do this one must recognize
> what is one's own—be familiar and at home with
> oneself. This means basically learning who one is,
> and learning what one has to offer to the contempo-
> rary world, and then learning how to make that of-
> fering valid.[26]

Interestingly, Merton goes on to make a link between the kind of experiential learning that leads to such self-knowl-edge and *salvation*. For him, discerning our personal calling seems to be equivalent to finding the path to salvation. This idea is as old as the Psalms: "Make me to know your ways, O Lord; teach me your paths. Lead me in your truth, and teach me, for you are the God of my salvation."[27]

But what *is* the secret to salvation? What path leads there? Asking such questions, we find ourselves in the position of the rich young man in the gospels who asked Jesus: "Good Teacher, what must I do to inherit eternal life?"[28] Although the man was apparently a solid citizen who kept out of trou-ble and followed all the rules, the story tells us that he went away sad because he was not prepared for the answer Jesus gave him: "Go, sell what you own, and give the money to the poor, and you will have treasure in heaven; then come, follow me." As the story goes, when the young man heard this, "he was shocked and went away grieving, for he had many pos-sessions." The implications of Jesus' shocking prescription for salvation will be explored in later chapters.

There are many ways to understand salvation, to imagine *how* we are saved and what we need to be saved *from*. The Christian tradition holds that one thing all of us need to be

saved from is *sin*. In the context of this exploration of vocation, it is useful to think of sin very broadly as encompassing
all of the various ways in which human beings say "No" to
the call of God. If vocation, as biblical scholar Walter Brueggemann has put it, is "finding a purpose for being in the world
which is related to the purposes of God," then sin is the pursuit of a personal purpose or agenda that is working at cross-
purposes with God.[29] We end up living in ways that are at
odds or out of tune with God's unique purpose or design for
our lives.[30]

The psychological parallel to the spiritual concept of sin
is *egocentrism*. "Psychologically," says John Sanford, "the egocentric state corresponds to the religious notion of original
sin, for it is a state of affairs from which we must be saved if
we are to live creatively and know God."[31] In general, ego-
centered inclinations can be seen as self-serving, self-promoting,
self-protective ways of thinking and feeling which incline us
toward life directions that are out of tune in some way with
the call of God. Unfortunately, our egos seem to be "hard-
wired" with this stubborn tendency to get caught up in superficial, inauthentic, selfish ways of being in the world.[32] In
contrast, when we are in tune with God and with the rhythms
and inclinations of our inmost self or conscience, our lives are
characterized by a progressive overcoming and surrender of
egocentric concerns, the fruits of which are evident in an
ever-deepening capacity for mature, authentic, and generous
love of God and other people.

According to Sanford, there are three kinds of life experiences that have the potential to save us by breaking down our
egocentricity. We can be changed or transformed, he says,
"through suffering, through the recognition of a power
greater than our own will at work in our lives, and by coming
to care for someone other than ourself."[33] One form of suffering is the kind of psychological pain and discomfort that often

accompanies any genuine process of emotional or spiritual growth. Becoming a conscious person, growing in self-knowledge, often requires that we find the courage to face uncomfortable, painful, or even embarrassing truths about ourselves that our fragile egos would prefer not to acknowledge or admit, even to ourselves.

Learning to love, becoming a loving person, also understandably stirs up considerable fear and resistance in our egos because opening ourselves to love is an inherently risky venture that makes us vulnerable to loss and hurt and disappointment. Mature love also often calls upon us to make the sacrifice of putting the needs of others before the needs and wishes of our own egos.

Finally, following the Voice ultimately requires that we let go of our own will or wishes in order to submit or surrender to the will of a power greater than our own ego—potentially at considerable personal cost. The most poignant example of this in the scriptures is Jesus' anguished prayer in the garden of Gethsemane: "Not my will, but yours be done."[34]

Sin and egocentrism, however, are not just individual matters. They are also social dimensions of sin and salvation. There are, for example, numerous forms of *social sin,* collective manifestations of selfishness that are harmful to the human community and the common good. Merton suggests that our individual salvation is integrally bound up with our participation in a wider collective process of healing and redemption of this troubled world in which we live. In a provocative reflection on the potential for higher education to contribute to such saving efforts, he writes:

> To put it in even more outrageous terms, the function of the university is to help men and women to save their souls and, in so doing, to save their society. From what? From the hell of meaninglessness, of obsession,

of complex artifice, of systematic lying, of criminal evasions and neglects, of self-destructive futilities.[35]

It is not hard to think of contemporary examples of the various social ills or "hells" on Merton's list. My students, for example, frequently express dismay about the sense of meaninglessness and emptiness in much of American popular culture; they worry about being seduced into mindless ways of living and working that are at odds with their deeper values and convictions. "Obsession" can be seen in the unhealthy patterns of overwork and overconsumption in American culture. These have given rise to an epidemic of "affluenza," which has been defined as "a painful, contagious, socially transmitted condition of overload, debt, anxiety, and waste resulting from the dogged pursuit of more."[36] Another American obsession is *national security*, which, especially since the 9/11 tragedy, has opened its own "Pandora's box" of complex artifice (trickery, pretense), systematic lying, criminal evasions and neglects, and self-destructive futilities in our country's conduct of the so-called "War on Terror." Some unique issues of conscience in the post-9/11 world will be examined in chapter 9.

In *Educating for Life: A Spiritual Vision for Every Teacher and Parent,* Thomas Groome suggests that we "consider the worthiest purpose of education as that learners might become fully alive human beings who help to create a society that serves the common good."[37] Any program or person in a position to teach or mentor young people can be of assistance in such "educating for life." In *Big Questions, Worthy Dreams,* Sharon Daloz Parks explores the potential for "mentoring communities" to help young adults grapple with the big questions of personal purpose, meaning, and social concern so that they may "discern a vision of the potential of life: *the world as it ought to be and the self as it might become.*"[38] This type of learning engages the whole person—not just the head but also the heart and soul of the learner. Thomas Moore calls it "deep education."[39]

"Education in this sense," says Merton, "means more than learning, and for such education, one is awarded no degree. One graduates by rising from the dead."[40] The kind of resurrection he is talking about, I think, is a process that potentially begins right here, right now, for each of us, while we are alive.

2

SACRED VOICES
Listen, So That You May Live

If reality speaks and God can speak in it, especially when it cries out, then listening to it is a necessary way of realizing our humanity.
    —Jon Sobrino, *Where Is God?*[1]

Why do you spend your money for that which is not bread, and your labor for that which does not satisfy? Listen carefully to me, and eat what is good, and delight yourselves in rich food. Incline your ear, and come to me; listen, so that you may live.
    —Isaiah 55:2–3

IN THE GOSPELS, there is often a great sense of urgency about Jesus and his message. It seems that Jesus wanted people to listen to him as if their very souls depended on it. In one memorable scene, he calls out to the crowd: "Let anyone with ears to hear *listen!*"[2] The people of first-century Galilee were blessed with the privilege of actually experiencing Jesus in person, and so his exhortation was quite straightforward: they were to incline their ears and hearts and minds in his direction and pay very careful attention, so as not to miss an incredible spiritual opportunity.

But what about us? Where do we listen for the Voice today? To what, or to whom, should we direct our attention? In this chapter I want to explore three fruitful places to listen for the sacred in the contemporary world. First, there are certain people we should listen to because God has a way of speaking to us through them. We hear echoes of the Voice in the words and deeds of all kinds of holy people, past and present, living or dead, who function as prophets or angels or messengers of God in our lives. They could include anyone from Jesus of Nazareth speaking to our hearts from across the centuries to a stranger we encountered on the subway this morning. The Voice is also calling to us all the time through the needs and sufferings of our fellow human beings; we hear it in the cry of the poor and the oppressed. Finally, if we listen very carefully, we can hear the "still, small voice" whispering within ourselves any time we want to hear it. In the words of Yeats, we "hear it in the deep heart's core."[3]

SPIRIT PERSONS

Certain gifted people are able to hear the Voice more distinctly than the rest of us; they have unusual gifts of hearing, special access to the sacred. Some are not only unusually in touch with the sacred, but also help to put the rest of us in touch with it as well. God has a way of speaking to us *through* their words and example. Theologian Marcus Borg has called such people "spirit persons."

The two primary characteristics of spirit persons, according to Borg, are their "vivid and frequent experiences of another level or dimension of reality" (such as hearing the voice of God) and their function as "mediators of the sacred" to the human community. "What they all have in common," says Borg, "is that they become funnels or conduits for the power or wisdom of God to enter this world."[4]

The founding figures of the great religious traditions are perhaps the clearest and most dramatic examples of spirit persons in human history. Sacred texts include striking accounts of sacred voices that were central to the call experiences of people such as Moses, Jesus, and Muhammad. "Moses! Moses!" cried the mysterious voice from the burning bush in the stirring account of how Moses was summoned to his own calling as the liberator of his people from oppression and bondage in Egypt.[5] "You are my beloved Son; with whom I am well pleased," said the tender voice to Jesus at the Jordan River, as his own identity and mission were becoming clear to himself and others.[6] "Read!" ordered the voice to the prophet Muhammad in the cave on Mount Hira, as he received the inspiration for the Q'uran and his call to become the messenger of Allah.[7]

Spirit persons are spiritual heroes. Considering Moses as an example of such spiritual heroism, John Sanford writes:

> The hero is the person whose consciousness becomes developed far beyond his fellows, whose psychological integration has been achieved, who fulfills in himself the divine plan and pattern for his life. By his greatly superior life and consciousness, the hero lifts the level of awareness and influences the history of a whole people.[8]

Spirit persons are encountered in all the major religious traditions of the world, including the most ancient form of spirituality, *shamanism*, which has been referred to as the "original religion" or the "oldest religion." Elements of shamanism are still practiced in the indigenous cultures of many areas of the world today. Dorcas, a traditional shamanic healer from southern Africa (known in her community as a *sangoma*), referred to spirit persons as people with "strong spirits" or "large spirits":

> The sangoma . . . is a person with a strong spirit. All people have a spirit, black people, white people, Chinese people, but God chooses some to talk through. It is like he gives some people a gift. All have spirit, but for some it is a gift, and those people become

sangomas. Like Jesus, do you know Jesus? God gave him a big, big gift, a large spirit. Many of the people didn't understand this about him. But he had that spirit. He walked alone in the mountains, didn't he? He talked with his spirits, didn't he? He made sick people better, didn't he? It is just like that. But you must go out—you must go out into the mountains, you know. How can you know anything if you don't go out? How can people learn about the spirits of the mountains and the rivers if you just go to the university? No, to learn about the spirits you must go out alone into the wild places.[9]

The title of this book comes from a song heard in a childhood vision of Black Elk, a great Native American visionary and healer in the shamanic tradition whose calling followed the pattern of persons who have vivid experiences of the sacred and who become mediators of the sacred to others. In *Black Elk Speaks*, he recalls the sacred voices he began to hear as a very young boy:

It was like somebody calling me, and I thought it was my mother, but there was nobody there. This happened more than once, and always made me afraid, so that I ran home. It was when I was five years old that my grandfather made me a bow and some arrows. The grass was young and I was horseback. A thunder storm was coming from where the sun goes down, and just as I was riding into the woods along a creek, there was a kingbird sitting on a limb. This was not a dream, it happened. And I was going to shoot at the kingbird with the bow my grandfather made, when the bird spoke and said: "The clouds all over are one-sided." Perhaps it meant that the clouds were looking at me. And then it said: "Listen! A voice is calling you!" Then I looked up at the clouds, and two men were coming there, headfirst like arrows slanting down; and as they came they sang a sacred song and the thunder was like drumming. I will sing it for you. The song and the drumming were like this:

> "Behold, a sacred voice is calling you;
> All over the sky a sacred voice is calling."[10]

Black Elk is also a striking example of someone who became a "funnel" or "conduit" for the power or wisdom of God to come into the world. In his case, he became a shamanic healer and leader among the Oglala Sioux people during a period of terrible crisis as their ancestral lands were being forcibly confiscated by the U.S. government in the latter half of the nineteenth century. In reflecting on his own powers to heal sick people (he refers to human beings as "two-leggeds" as opposed to the animals or "four-leggeds"), Black Elk displays his deep humility and spiritual insight, seeing himself as a channel or "hole" through which the healing power of God can flow into the world:

> I had the power to practice as a medicine man, curing sick people, and many I cured through the power that came through me. Of course it was not I who cured. It was the power from the outer world, and the visions and ceremonies had only made me like a hole through which the power could come through to the two-leggeds. If I thought that I was doing it myself, the hole would close up and no power could come through. Then everything I could do would be foolish.[11]

Following the 9/11 tragedy, I experienced a calling to learn more about the spiritual tradition of Islam. I discovered that the prophet Muhammad also strikingly embodies the pattern of the spirit person. His unique calling was to become the "messenger of Allah," one who would deliver God's message by serving as a vessel through which the inspired wisdom of the Q'uran would come into the world. The story of Muhammad's call experience is worth considering in some detail.

Little is known of Muhammad's life prior to his call experience except that he was an orphan (he later had a reputation for special kindness to orphans), that he apparently never learned to read and write, and that at some point he became a fairly successful merchant and settled with his wife and children in the town of Mecca on the Arabian peninsula.[12] When he was about forty years old, he began to regularly spend time in prayer and solitude, sometimes making spiritual retreats in the hills around Mecca. Around this time he also began a regular practice of distributing food to the poor (prayer and almsgiving would later become central to the practice of Islam).

In the year 610, while praying in a cave on Mount Hira near Mecca, Muhammad had a vivid experience of the sacred that signaled the beginning of his own prophetic vocation. "The Truth descended upon him when he was in the cave at Hira," reads the *Hadith*. Accounts suggest that Muhammad had a spiritual encounter with a terrifying angelic presence that ordered him to "Read!" ("Recite!" in other translations). It was as if he was being ordered to read or recite the beginning verses of the Q'uran in the moment they were first being revealed to him. "I do not know how to read," he protested. The angel was very insistent and did not accept his repeated protests and excuses about being unable to read, and the account goes on to describe an intense, exhausting, violent struggle between Muhammad and the angel that is reminiscent of Jacob's wrestling match with his own dark angelic adversary in the Book of Genesis.[13] Finally, in spite of his re-

sistance and fear, Muhammad surrenders to the inspiration
and to his prophetic vocation as the one who will bring it
into the world: "Then the Prophet returned with the Inspiration and with his heart beating severely."[14] After this experience, several years of careful, patient work were required for
Muhammad to fully receive the inspiration and to dictate the
verses of the Q'uran to someone who could write them
down.

Larger-than-life historic persons like Muhammad and
Black Elk provide dramatic examples of persons with unusual
mystical gifts who become mediators of the sacred to others.
It is important to remember, however, that a spirit person can
be *anyone* who mediates the sacred to us, who serves in some
way as a prophet or an angel or a messenger of God in our
lives. *Prophet*, in Hebrew, means "mouthpiece" of God, and
angel means "messenger." It might be that a very ordinary person in the circle of our everyday life, a family member or
friend or co-worker or neighbor, turns out to be the spirit
person who delivers a personal message to us from God. It
could be someone who serves as a prophetic truthteller in our
life, who "tells it like it is," who shakes us up and challenges us
to think about our life priorities in a new way. It could also be
someone who appears as an angel of mercy in a time of pain
or need, who speaks just the consoling words we need to hear
in a moment of discouragement, or who gives us just the kind
of advice or perspective we need in a time of personal confusion or darkness.

The spiritual challenge, according to Margaret Guenther,
is to *get* the message, to recognize and appreciate spirit persons when they come along:

> The big question...is how do we recognize the an-
> gels who come to us in our everyday lives. They are
> easy to identify in works of art, in stained glass win-
> dows and Christmas cards. But how many do we miss

in the ordinary course of our days because of our inattention or willful resistance?[15]

Finally, it is important to remember that *strangers* sometimes serve as spirit persons in our lives. "Do not neglect to show hospitality to strangers," says the writer of the Letter to the Hebrews, "for by doing that some have entertained angels without knowing it."[16] Recognition of the spiritual potential of encounters with strangers is also found in early Celtic Christianity:

I saw a stranger yesterday;
I put food in the eating place,
drink in the drinking place,
music in the listening place;
and in the sacred name of the Triune God
he blessed myself and my house,
my cattle and my dear ones,
and the lark said in her song:
Often, Often, Often, goes the Christ in a stranger's
   guise.[17]

THE CRY OF THE POOR

One of the most privileged and sacred places where the Voice can be discerned today is in the needs and sufferings of our fellow human beings. We hear it by listening with an open heart to the cry of the poor and the oppressed.

God is always trying to get us to pay attention to the scandal of unjust poverty, the deprivations of basic human rights (enough food to survive and thrive, decent housing, education, medical care) that are the daily reality of most of our brothers and sisters in the world. Although there are many kinds of need and suffering, the particular focus here is on those who are materially or economically poor. There are also many degrees of poverty in differing circumstances in various areas of the world.[18] For our purposes, economic and social statistics will be less useful than an appreciation of the personal experience or meaning of poverty to the poor themselves. Leonardo and Clodovis Boff, a pair of theologians from Brazil who happen to be brothers, offer this definition of poverty from the perspective of the poor: "'Poor' for the people means dependence, debt, exposure, anonymity, contempt, and humiliation."[19]

Jon Sobrino, a Jesuit theologian from El Salvador whose writings focus relentlessly on the problem of social suffering, says we must "hear the word of reality," particularly the message that comes to us from the reality of people who are needlessly suffering in unjust poverty. Cornel West, a professor of African American studies and religion at Princeton University, also writes of the painful truth of social suffering and the challenge of "allowing the suffering to speak":

> We have to keep track, at any given moment, of who is bearing most of the social cost. This is what it means to look at the world from the vantage point of those below. I believe, in fact, that the condition of truth is to allow the suffering to speak. It doesn't mean that those who suffer have a monopoly on truth, but it means that the condition of truth to emerge must be in tune with those who are undergoing social misery —socially induced forms of suffering.[20]

Frantz Fanon, an Algerian psychiatrist who wrote passionately and furiously about the injustice of European colonialism in Africa and the revolutionary struggles of the people of his native Algeria against it, referred to the poor and oppressed as "the wretched of the earth."[21] Nelson Maldonado Torres writes

eloquently about the theme of the "cry" of the wretched of the
earth in Fanon's writings:

> The cry is, indeed, precisely that, a sound uttered as a
> call for attention, as a demand for immediate action
> or remedy, or as an expression of pain that points to
> an injustice committed or to something that is lack-
> ing. The cry is the revelation of someone who has
> been forgotten or wronged.[22]

We are called to hear the cries of the wretched of the
earth today just as God heard the cry of the Israelites in ancient Egypt: "The Israelites groaned under their slavery, and
cried out. Out of the slavery their cry for help rose up to
God. God heard their groaning."[23] Interestingly, the Exodus
story tells us that God heard and responded to the Israelites'
cries for help through a human being, Moses:

> Then the LORD said, "I have observed the misery of
> my people who are in Egypt; I have heard their cry
> on account of their taskmasters. Indeed, I know their
> sufferings, and I have come down to deliver them
> from the Egyptians, and to bring them up out of that
> land to a good and broad land, a land flowing with
> milk and honey.... The cry of the Israelites has now
> come to me; I have also seen how the Egyptians op-
> press them. So come, I will send you to Pharaoh to
> bring my people, the Israelites, out of Egypt."[24]

The Exodus story gives us a glimpse of the heart of a
God who hears the cries of the oppressed and who intends to
do something to help them, but it also gives us a glimpse into
the heart of Moses. "It's not right!" is the natural response of
the heart to injustice and inhumanity, a feeling response that
usually consists of some combination of compassionate feel-

ing for the sufferers and indignation that they should have to
be in such a situation in the first place.[25] In the Exodus story,
God is moved to compassion and indignation by the plight of
the Israelites, a response that seems to be mirrored or echoed
in the compassion and indignation of Moses in response to
his people's misery. We know that Moses was a man capable
of violent passion because, prior to his call experience, he had
flown into a rage and killed an Egyptian taskmaster who was
abusing an Israelite slave. After his calling, Moses was required
to channel his great compassion and indignation into the
service of the higher purpose of liberating his people from
their oppression.

One of the most important ways in which we hear or
register the cry of the poor is through listening to the response of our own hearts to their pain and need. In order to
have eyes to see and ears to hear, we must also have hearts
that feel. Hardness or numbness of heart, which is manifested
in a *lack* of appropriate human feeling for social suffering, results in impaired hearing. The consequent obliviousness to
the suffering of the poor is a great spiritual danger, especially
for privileged people. Paul Farmer, an American doctor who
has tirelessly devoted his career to caring for the urban poor
in the United States and the rural poor in Haiti, the poorest
country in the Western hemisphere, writes with dismay about
this widespread inability to see and hear the poor:

> The voices, the faces, the suffering of the sick and the
> poor are all around us. Can we see and hear them?
> Well-defended against troubling incursions of doubt,
> we the privileged are precisely the people most at
> risk of remaining oblivious, since this kind of suffer-
> ing is not central to our own experience.[26]

One practical remedy for obliviousness to the suffering of
the poor is regular personal contact with the poor. Dean

Brackley focuses on the spiritual potential of personal contact
with victims of oppression to put us in touch not only with
the reality of human misery but also with the mysterious
mercy of God. Brackley teaches at the University of Central
America in El Salvador, where he volunteered to replace one
of the martyred Jesuits after six members of the Jesuit faculty
were murdered by the Salvadoran military in November
1989. In an essay called "Meeting the Victims, Falling in Love,"
he writes:

> These people shake us up because they bring home
> to us that things are much worse in the world than
> we dared to imagine. . . . It seems that the victim of-
> fers us the privileged place (although not the only
> place) to encounter the truth that sets us free. The
> poor usher us into the heart of reality. . . . The victims
> of history—the destitute, abused women, oppressed
> minorities, all those the Bible calls "the poor"—not
> only put us in touch with the world and with our-
> selves, but also with the mercy of God. There is
> something fathomless about the encounter with the
> poor. . . . If we let them, the poor will place us before
> the abyss of the holy Mystery we call God. They are
> a kind of door that opens before that Mystery and
> through which God passes to get at us.[27]

THE STILL, SMALL VOICE

Finally, if we listen very carefully, it is possible to hear the
"still, small voice" whispering to us from within ourselves.

The image of the still, small voice resonates deeply with
many people. It seems to capture something of the depth and
nuance and mystery of the inner voice, the patience and
practice it takes to hear it, and our intuition that there really

is something *worth* listening for beneath all the noise and activity on the surface of our lives. The image of the "still, small voice" comes from a mysterious story about the prophet Elijah in the First Book of Kings:

> And there he came to a cave, and lodged there; and behold, the word of the Lord came to him, and said to him, "What are you doing here, Elijah?" ... And behold, the Lord passed by, and a great and strong wind rent the mountains, and broke in pieces the rocks before the Lord, but the Lord was not in the wind; and after the wind an earthquake, but the Lord was not in the earthquake; and after the earthquake a fire, but the Lord was not in the fire; and after the fire a *still, small voice.* And when Elijah heard it, he hid his face in his mantle and went out and stood at the entrance of the cave. And behold, there came a voice to him, and said, "What are you doing here, Elijah?"[28]

For our purposes, the background of the story is less important than the way its rich symbolism speaks to us today. The clear implication is that, like Elijah, we may tend to look for God in the wrong places, in the noisy or dramatic experiences of life, in the wind or the earthquake or the fire. But according to the story, the Lord is not "in" these places where we might expect to find him. Rather, the Spirit may unexpectedly be found in other kinds of experiences, perhaps speaking in a quieter, softer, subtler tone that we are likely to miss if we are not paying attention, or if we are mistakenly directing our attention someplace else. And so we must learn to listen in a discerning way, and in the right places, for the mysterious whispering of the Spirit.

Learning to sit still, to calm and quiet ourselves enough to be able to hear something other than the surface noise of

our lives or the distracting inner chatter of our own egos, is a
necessary prerequisite for being able to detect the stirrings of
the still, small voice.[29] James Hillman writes: "Prayer has been
described as an active silence in which one listens acutely for
the still small voice, as if prayer were not asking and getting
through to God, but becoming so composed that He might
come through to me."[30] There are many things that can get in
the way of our composing ourselves and sitting still long
enough to hear something other than the usual racket. The
still, small voice gets crowded out and drowned out by too
much hectic *doing* and not enough *being,* too much extro-
verted activity and too little of the kind of relaxed solitude
and leisure that are essential to developing a spiritual life. "To
listen for God is a countercultural enterprise," says Margaret
Guenther, "for much in our lives works against the patient
labor of attentiveness."[31] Such attentiveness requires that we
find or make time away from what John Boyle O'Reilly
called "the street's rude bustle":

> Oh, no, from the street's rude bustle,
> From the trophies of mart and stage,
> I would fly to the wood's low rustle
> And the meadow's kindly page.[32]

Time-honored practices of prayer and meditation can be
seen as techniques for improving our listening skills so that
we are able to listen more consciously and intentionally for
the still, small voice. Although prayer is popularly understood
as *talking* to God, true dialogue with any other person, including God, consists of a mutual exchange that allows both
partners opportunities to speak *and* listen. "Every prayer,"
writes Friedrich Heiler, "is a turning [of the human person]
to another Being to whom they inwardly open their heart; it
is the speech of an 'I' to a 'Thou.'"[33] True prayer not only allows us to address the divine "Thou," but also makes it possi-

ble for the sacred Other to address *us*. If our prayer consists of too much talking and not enough listening, if it is so full of ourselves that little or no room is left for God, it becomes a one-sided, self-centered monologue rather than a real personal dialogue or encounter.

A common obstacle to such prayerful dialogue is the thought that there is really no one on the other end of our prayer, that prayer is actually just a matter of talking to *ourselves*. On some level, we may buy into the Freudian view that prayer is a form of wishful thinking or childish fantasy. From this perspective, the belief that there is a God who is interested in a personal relationship with us—who actually listens to and answers our prayers—is seen as a comforting illusion for people who are unable to stand on their own two feet. On the other hand, the opposite concern—a fear that there might really be Someone or Something on the other end of our prayer—can also become an obstacle, another reason to avoid silence and listening. "There is a reason...that more people do not find the silence and listen to the inner voice," says John Sanford. "They are afraid to do so. The truth is that in our culture we fear silence precisely because something from within *might* speak to us."[34]

On a psychological level, prayer is like listening to the *unconscious*. It is a way of focusing attention on our inner emotional experience so as to establish a dialogue or connection with our inner self. Conscious self-awareness facilitates the dialogue between the unconscious and the conscious mind by making the unconscious *conscious*. In psychological terms, avoidance of prayerful silence is a kind of defensive maneuver to avoid the uncomfortable experience of learning things about ourselves that we would prefer not to know. Sanford writes:

> We prefer the noise and fear the silence because in that silence the unconscious might make its presence felt. This unconscious will contain all that we have

been repressing and denying about ourselves. It is impossible, therefore, to learn to listen to the still, small voice within, without also coming to terms with the unconscious.[35]

Our ability to hear the inner voice can also be limited by a lack of imagination. The idea that God might actually speak to us personally—that there actually is such a thing as a "still, small voice"—requires some religious imagination. In an insightful little book titled *God Is More Present than You Think*, Robert Ochs suggests that, with a little religious imagination, *all* of our life experiences can be seen as potential means for encountering God, as ways for God to communicate with us.[36] From this perspective, the experience of a helpful thought coming into our consciousness when we are struggling with a personal problem can be interpreted not just as our own thought, but as the *answer* to a prayer. The thought is something that is spoken *to* us within our mind by God, who *gives* us the thought in order to help us with our problem. During an emotionally trying time, the consoling thought that "No matter what happens, God still loves me" can be taken as God's personal communication of reassurance *to* us.

It takes an unusual imaginative effort for many of us to imagine that God actually loves us. One helpful way to discern whether a particular thought or message comes from God is to assess whether it seems to be accompanied by a loving, emotional tone. Does it sound like the kind of thing someone who loves us might say? Spiritual writer Henri Nouwen has suggested that the essence of prayer is learning to listen deep within ourselves for the consoling inner voice of love.[37] The idea is that each human person has the potential to hear something like the tender, affirming voice that Jesus is said to have heard at the moment of his baptism in the Jordan River, a voice that assured him of how much he was loved by and pleasing to God.[38] Before moving on, it is worth pausing to consider Nouwen's view of prayer:

> I have read and written much about prayer, but when I go to a quiet place to pray, I realize that, although I have a tendency to say many things to God, the real "work" of prayer is to become silent and listen to the voice that says good things about me. This might sound self-indulgent, but, in practice, it is a hard discipline.... Have you ever tried to spend a whole hour doing nothing but listening to the voice that dwells deep in your heart?... It is not easy to enter into the silence and reach beyond the many boisterous and demanding voices of our world and to discover there the small intimate voice saying: "You are my beloved child...."[39]

3

DISCERNMENT
The Inner Compass of the Heart

Ah, but how to give oneself away? How do we discover what our particular self-gift, our vocation, is? Or, to put it another way, how do we discern the will of God for us?
—Michael Himes[1]

There are all different kinds of voices calling you . . . and the problem is to find out which is the voice of God rather than of Society, say, or the Superego, or Self-Interest.
—Frederick Buechner[2]

LISTENING FOR THE VOICE OF VOCATION, we inevitably encounter a conflicting mix of voices within ourselves and in our world that beckon us in many possible directions. Which of these we allow to influence our choices will have profound implications, for better or for worse, not only for the quality of our own lives, but also for the future well-being of our loved ones, our communities, and the wider world.

What criteria should we use to tell the difference between the still, small voice of the Spirit and all the other distracting, competing noises in ourselves and our world that are clamoring for our attention at any given moment? How is it possible to differentiate between the real and the counterfeit, between the call of conscience and the voices of conformity and convention? For James Joyce, the issue was how to distinguish between the "call of life to the soul" and the "dull, gross voice of the world of duties and despair."[3]

In this chapter I want to explore a number of dimensions of discernment, beginning with a look at the affective dimensions of what an authentic sense of vocation *feels* like to people who are trying to discern and follow their callings. Along the way, the traditional spiritual criteria for "discernment of spirits" will be examined, along with some modern psychological parallels to these older spiritual guidelines for finding our way. I also want to make some connections between personal calling and social responsibility, vocational discernment and social analysis. Discernment pertains to more than just our efforts to evaluate and interpret the complex crosscurrents of our inner experience. It also involves cultivating a critical consciousness about our social reality so that we can discover our social responsibilities within it and decide how best to use our energies and talents for the common good.

THE INNER COMPASS

At important crossroads in our lives, we are faced with the challenge of finding our bearings in order to make decisions about whether one particular route or another will best get us to where we want to go. Discernment has to do with our ability to find the path that leads in the right direction.

Psychologist William Sheldon has suggested that there is a kind of hunger or "craving" in the human psyche for a sense of orientation or direction that will lead us to authentic health and happiness:

> Psychologists well know that the deepest element of human happiness is embodied in the idea of movement toward something; movement in the "right"

direction; and all of the devices of therapeutic psychiatry are really only shoves and pushes and suggestions
intended to help a mind find its particular right direction of movement. Continued observation of the
basic dynamic nature of happiness, especially in clinical psychological practice, leads almost invariably to
the conclusion that deeper and more fundamental than
sexuality, deeper than the craving for social power,
deeper even than the desire for possession, there is a
still more generalized and more universal craving in
the human make-up. It is the craving for knowledge of
the right direction—or orientation.[4]

When we move in the right direction, we feel right with
God and with ourselves. Inwardly, we experience the sense of
intuitive "rightness" that accompanies any step we take in the
direction of emotional and spiritual health and growth. We
feel healthy when we are moving in the right direction; the
path feels right to us.

The affective promptings of our inner self help to orient
and guide us on the path to healing, wholeness, and meaning.
"The self is the principle and archetype of orientation and
meaning," wrote Jung. "Therein lies its healing function."[5]
More and more, it seems to me that the central task of both
psychotherapy and vocational discernment is to get oriented,
to find a healthy and fitting and proper sense of direction.
Such a sense of direction emerges only through careful and
thoughtful consideration of all the options before us in order
to determine whether they are in tune with the inclinations
of the deeper self.

On a psychological level, the inner voice makes itself
known through the emotional urgings and resistances of our
own hearts. We hear a "yes" or "no" from within our very
beings about whether a path is right for us. On a spiritual

level, when we move in the right direction we have the experience of "consolation." This is the word Saint Ignatius Loyola used to describe the consoling feelings of inner peace and joy that stir within us when we are living in tune with God's will. On the other hand, when we move in the wrong direction, we experience a sense of inner darkness or "desolation." Ignatius, who in the sixteenth century developed a psychologically sophisticated system of spiritual discernment that is still in use today, had the simple but profound insight that we can discern where God is calling or leading us through careful attention to the movements and inclinations of our own hearts. He believed that our hearts can be used as a kind of inner compass to tell us whether the directions we are considering are consistent with the ways in which God would have us go.[6]

Ignatius believed that human beings are capable of moving in two fundamental directions: *toward* God or *away* from God. In *Listening to the Music of the Spirit,* David Lonsdale provides a helpful summary of the Ignatian view of how our feelings can give us important information about where we stand in relation to God:

> The practice of discernment relies on the fact that all the different dimensions of the human person are interconnected and interact with each other. When, at the deepest level of being, we move toward God or in opposition to God, this movement has its repercussions in our affective life: our conscious feelings, moods, and desires are touched. Similarly in the other direction: when our feelings are stirred by our experience of the world around us, this has its repercussions at the deeper level of how we actually stand in relation to God. Thus our affective movements and responses, which we can relatively easily be aware of and name,

are signs of how we actually stand in relation to God
at a deeper, more hidden level of ourselves.[7]

Because feelings are potentially such a valuable resource
in direction-finding, we must become comfortable and at
home in the world of our inner emotional experience. Learning to acknowledge and name our feelings makes it possible
for us to use them consciously in our decision-making. This is
good not only for our emotional health but also for our spiritual health, because it helps us know whether we are living in
tune with God.

DISCERNMENT OF SPIRITS

The idea that unseen forces or spirits can have a powerful influence on the emotional and physical health, well-being, and
behavior of human beings was widespread in the ancient
world and persists in many cultures to the present day. This
belief has been particularly prominent in the spirituality and
healing practices of shamanism.[8] Belief in spirits was also
common in the world of the New Testament, as is evidenced
in the gospel accounts of Jesus' dialogues with Satan and in
the stories of Jesus' healing encounters with people who were
seen as being possessed by demonic or "unclean" spirits.

In sixteenth-century Europe, Ignatius Loyola also believed
that different movements or inclinations of the soul (feelings,
thoughts, fantasies, desires) were associated with the hidden
influence of "good" and "evil" spirits. In his view, evil spirits
(Satan, the devil) work to tempt or pull us *away* from God,
while good spirits (or the Holy Spirit) work to draw or incline us *toward* God. Although the good versus evil distinction
may initially appear simplistic, Ignatius was well aware of the
complexities of discernment in real-life decision-making, and

he developed his own set of guidelines for recognizing and interpreting the movements of spirits in the human soul. A passage from Nikos Kazantzakis's novel *The Last Temptation of Christ* captures some of the ambiguity inherent in this process:

> "Someone came last night in my sleep," he murmured under his breath, as though he feared the visitor were still there and might overhear him. "Someone came. Surely it was God, God...or was it the devil? Who can tell them apart? They exchange faces, God sometimes becomes all darkness, the devil all light, and the mind of man is left in a muddle." There were two paths. Which way should he go, which path should he choose?[9]

The terminology of "spirits" is awkward for modern, psychologically minded people. In his commentary on *Spiritual Exercises of St. Ignatius,* David Fleming reminds us that, for Ignatius, "the words 'good' and 'evil' as applied to 'spirits' are used primarily to designate the kind of movement or feeling in terms of its *direction* or *goal*."[10] Although many people have difficulty with the idea of the existence of invisible spirits, most of us can intuitively appreciate the distinction between different types of motivations or desires that incline us in markedly different directions. We can also recognize that the choices we make to follow one particular inclination over another may have very different outcomes—for better or for worse—in terms of our emotional and spiritual health and growth.

Contemporary psychological language for "spirits" might make a distinction between "ego-centered" versus "God-centered" inclinations. What has traditionally been associated with the evil spirit can be understood as having to do with *ego-centered inclinations* that draw us into increasing egocentrism and alienation from God, others, and ourselves. Ego-centered inclinations are self-serving, self-promoting, self-protective ways of feeling and thinking that incline us toward ways of living that are out of tune with the call of God and with the deeper rhythms and desires of our authentic self. If we follow them, we are likely to get caught up in the kind of empty, superficial, inauthentic, self-centered ways of living that have traditionally been known as sin. Self-protection and self-gratification (personal ambition, comfort, security, pleasure, status, control, wealth, etc.) become more important than love for God or others.[11] A character in Iris Murdoch's novel *The Black Prince* describes the essence of egocentrism:

> The natural tendency of the human soul is towards the protection of the ego. The Niagara-like force of this tendency can be readily recognized by introspection, and its results are everywhere on public show. We desire to be richer, handsomer, cleverer, stronger, more adored and more apparently good than anyone else. . . . The burden of genuine goodness is instinctively appreciated as intolerable, and a desire for it would put out of focus the other and ordinary wishes by which one lives.[12]

God-centered inclinations, on the other hand, are desires that draw us into deeper, authentic, loving connection with God, others, and ourselves.[13] Such inclinations lead us in directions that are in tune with the call of God and with the deepest and truest desires of our authentic self. God's love and truth are the top priority. Being true to ourselves by considering whether something is the loving or authentic thing to do becomes the most important criterion in our choices. The distinction between ego-centered and God-centered desires will be discussed further in the next chapter.

THREE KEY QUESTIONS

In *Doing the Truth in Love*, Michael Himes suggests three key questions to consider in vocational discernment and decision-making.[14] The questions center around *joy*, *talent*, and *service*. An authentic calling brings together three things: what we most enjoy doing, what we are good at, and what others most need from us.

The first question to consider in discerning whether a path or activity is right for us is whether we experience a sense of joy when we are doing it (or thinking about doing it). This requires a capacity to observe ourselves, to notice how we are feeling as we engage in the activity or as we imagine engaging in it. Himes makes an important qualitative distinction between *joy*, which he sees as a deep and reliable internal indicator of spiritual rightness, and *happiness*, a feeling that is more transient and superficial and dependent on external factors:

> Thus whether or not a particular way of living or working makes you feel happy is irrelevant to the discernment of vocation. But whether or not it is a source of joy, a profound conviction that it is a good way to live a life and spend one's energy and talent, is of immense significance.[15]

It is possible, for example, to experience a sense of quiet joy in our souls about the overall direction of our love or work life (e.g., about becoming a doctor or the rightness of a life-long commitment to one's spouse) even if things are not particularly easy or pleasant at any given moment (e.g., we are in the midst of a stressful period of medical training, or we just had a difference of opinion with our husband or wife).

In the Christian tradition, joy is one of the "fruits of the Spirit."[16] Ignatius Loyola's early insights about discernment came to him during a period of convalescence after a leg injury when he had a lot of time to think about his future and to notice the different kinds of feelings that various options or possibilities evoked in him. One of the most important things he began to notice was a qualitative difference between the kinds of joy or happiness that seemed to be associated with different kinds of desires and fantasies about his future. He ended up resolving to pursue the options that promised the deepest and most lasting sense of joy.[17]

The next question to consider is whether we possess the talent or ability to do a particular thing. "For reasons that are as mysterious as the wellsprings of the self," says Sam Keen, "each of us is predisposed to be good at certain things and poor at others."[18] A true calling recognizes our unique God-given personal gifts and talents and finds ways to put them to good use:

> Now there are varieties of gifts, but the same Spirit; and there are varieties of services, but the same Lord; and there are varieties of activities, but it is the same God who activates all of them in everyone. To each is given the manifestation of the Spirit for the common good.[19]

The central question is "What am I good at?" or "What is my gift?" Answering a question like this requires a realistic sense of the things we do well and the things that we don't do so well. Sometimes feedback from others (e.g., affirmation of our gifts from a respected mentor) can help us to recognize our strengths and weaknesses in various areas. Experiences of failure too can teach us important lessons about our limitations or weaknesses. A willingness to experiment, to test out our abilities and skills in the real world, is also helpful in discerning whether our dreams and aspirations are realistic and achievable. Do we possess the necessary skills, talents, interests, and personality traits to successfully pursue this calling? If not, can we cultivate them or acquire them through training, discipline, and practice? We usually do better at tasks, activities, and pursuits that come naturally (not necessarily easily) and that we spontaneously find interesting and enjoyable. We also tend to be happier in work that is suited to our temperament or personality. A sense of "fit" accompanies a true calling.

The final question has to do with the common good. "The sense of vocation," says Keen, "arises at the point where a crying need, a call, an appeal seems to be addressed to us that we can only answer by sharing the endowments, talents, and skills we have been given."[20] After considering whether something is a source of joy and whether we have the talent for it, we must ask whether our doing it would be of any real help or service to people in the real world. Would it usefully address a human need or make a helpful contribution to the world in any way? These questions cannot be answered in isolation, but only in consultation with others. Whether something is useful to other people is perhaps a judgment made more appropriately by others—maybe even by the community that would be the recipient of the service. "Others may not need to be served *in this way*," Himes reminds us, "or to be served in this way by *you*."[21] The challenge is to discern the unique manifestation of the Spirit that each of us has been given for the common good.

DISCERNMENT AND SOCIAL ANALYSIS

Discernment is not only a matter of personal reflection and self-analysis. It also has collective dimensions. Just as we attempt to discern the spirits and inclinations within ourselves, we must also evaluate the origins and aims of the forces and trends operating in our social world. We must read the signs of the times in order to differentiate between the authentic voice of vocation and what Buechner calls "the great, blaring, boring, banal voice of mass culture."[22] Our ability to size up and critique our social reality helps us to discern our social responsibilities within it, and helps us figure out how to best use our energies and talents for the common good.

Socially responsible discernment includes social analysis, which has to do with a critical or discerning consciousness about the world in which we live. Social analysis does not require advanced education or specialized knowledge in political science or sociology or liberation theology. According to Dan Hartnett, it is actually more about the "practical wisdom" of regular people who have taken the trouble to educate themselves about their social world. This involves a more ordinary human exercise of critical reflection "whereby the educated adult remains critically attuned to what is happening in the world in order to think, judge, and act responsibly."[23]

Joe Holland and Peter Henriot describe social analysis as the effort to obtain a more complete picture of our social situation by exploring its *historical* and *structural* dimensions.[24] To develop insight into social structures, says Hartnett, we must become "proficient question raisers."[25] In a nutshell, to grasp the history of any particular situation we must begin by asking good questions that help us to appreciate how and why things came to be the way they are. Understanding the structural dimension, on the other hand, has to do with asking questions that help in getting a handle on the forces and factors and attitudes that *keep* things the way they are.

Socially responsible discernment involves understanding social structures that oppress the poor, asking questions about how people came to be poor, about what *makes* them poor and *keeps* them poor. The answers to such questions can help us to figure out what can and should be done to change things. In *Pedagogy of the Oppressed,* the influential Brazilian educator Paolo Freire referred to the process of developing our capacity for critical consciousness as *conscientizaçao* (Portuguese for "consciousness-raising"; in Spanish, *concientización*). "The term *conscientizaçao*," wrote Freire, "refers to learning to perceive social, political, and economic contradictions, and to take action against the oppressive elements of reality."[26] Assisting people in their efforts to develop their capacity for critical consciousness and empowering them to take responsible action to liberate themselves from oppressive situations is what liberation theology and the "option for the poor" are all about. "The church's option," says Leonardo Boff, "is a preferential option for the poor, against their poverty."[27] (See the section entitled "Option for the Poor" in chapter 9 of this book.)

Social analysis follows a simple, three-step methodology: *observe, judge, act.*[28] The "observe" part of the formula begins with careful looking and listening in order to perceive the particular situation as fully and clearly as we can. It has to do with developing "eyes to see" and "ears to hear." The "judge" part of the formula involves rendering judgment or a critique based on careful observation. We may begin with a global judgment: "We look at the lives of the poor," says Paul Farmer, "and are sure, just as they are, that *something is terribly wrong.*"[29] The task is then to clarify and refine our diagnosis of exactly what is wrong and why. Finally, the "act" part of the formula involves using our insights and judgments in the service of social change—to "take action against the oppressive elements of reality." Using medical terminology, accurate assessment and diagnosis will guide our intervention and treatment of the unhealthy social situation.

An important element of social analysis has to do with our capacity to question and critically examine our own *social position* or location in the world. Though we may be a "good person" who means well, justice still requires that we take a hard look at the ways we may be unconsciously participating in, supporting, or benefiting from an unjust status quo that gives unfair, unearned advantages to privileged persons in our society (e.g., because we are white, or male, of a certain social class, etc.). It is necessary for us to do this so we can break free of cultural and institutional patterns of ignorance and complacency that hold us back from being truly just and compassionate persons.

The very different vocational prospects for the "haves" and the "have nots" in our world offer a good starting point for the process of critical reflection on our social position. We should consider, for example, the question of whether the intricacies of vocational discernment are just a luxury for the privileged classes who are economically secure enough to be able to worry about things like "authenticity" or "following their bliss." While a small minority of the world's population is blessed with a range of interesting career options to choose from, the poor are cursed with severely limited options. For most of the world's people, extreme poverty closes off vocational possibilities for meaningful work. The poor are consequently less concerned with whether a job is "right" for them and more with whether there is any kind of job for them at all.

Various forms of discrimination also painfully complicate the vocational picture for people who are "different" in one way or another because of their race, social class, religion, ethnicity, gender, sexual orientation, or any other category of difference that may affect their chances in life. Many people are denied the right or opportunity to pursue their callings and fulfill their God-given potential simply *because* they are different, i.e., they are the "wrong" skin color or religion, or poor, or members of an unpopular ethnic group, or women, or gay, or whatever. The frustrated callings and deferred dreams that result from such discrimination are the cause of widespread emotional and social misery. According to Bishop Desmond Tutu, victims of injustice and prejudice are also at risk for developing a deeper kind of spiritual problem: "One of the most blasphemous consequences of injustice and prejudice," he says, "is that it can make a child of God doubt that he or she is a child of God."[30]

Examining our particular social position or location in the scheme of things can also help us to discern the particular social responsibilities we are personally called to take on. "Discerning our social location within a web of economic, political, and cultural systems," says Mary Elizabeth Hobgood, "is essential to evaluating our responsibility to others."[31] It may even be that privileged people are called to carry a *greater* burden of social responsibility: "From everyone to whom much has been given," said Jesus, "much will be required."[32]

People to whom much has been given might do well to think in terms of *giving things back* that didn't actually belong to them in the first place. According to Walter Brueggemann, this is consistent with the biblical meaning of justice:

> Let me offer this as a way the Bible thinks about justice: *Justice is to sort out what belongs to whom, and to return it to them.* Such an understanding implies that there is a right distribution of goods and access to the sources of life. There are certain entitlements which cannot be mocked. Yet through uneven workings of the historical process, some come to have access to or control of what belongs to others. If we control what rightly belongs to others long enough, we come to think of it as rightly ours, and to forget it belongs to someone else. And so the work of liberation, redemption, salvation is *giving things back.*[33]

One way to keep "giving things back" in mind is to always ask ourselves how any particular choice or decision we make will affect the poor. Paul Farmer puts the question this way: "How is this relevant to the suffering of the poor and to the relief of that suffering?"[34] Cultivating the habit of asking such questions in our vocational discernment is a form of spiritual discipline that potentially puts us in touch with great spiritual energy and power. It can become like a *talisman* (a spiritually powerful object worn or carried for protection from evil) that we carry with us at all times. Here is what is known as "Gandhi's talisman":

> I will give you a talisman. Whenever you are in doubt, or when the self becomes too much with you, apply the following test. Recall the face of the poorest and the weakest person whom you have seen, and ask yourself if the next step you contemplate is going to be of any use to that person. Will that person gain anything by it? Will it restore that person to control over his or her own life or destiny? In other words, will it lead to freedom for the hungry and spiritually starving millions? Then you will find your doubts and your self melting away.[35]

4

AUTHENTICITY
To Live as though the Truth Were True

Our deepest calling is to grow into our authentic selfhood.
—Parker Palmer[1]

To open ourselves to the truth and to bring ourselves face to face with our personal and collective reality is not an option that can be accepted or rejected. It is an undeniable requirement of all people and all societies that seek to humanize themselves and to be free.
—Bishop Juan Gerardi[2]

IN SHAKESPEARE'S *HAMLET*, Polonius offers his son Laertes what has become famous advice: "This above all: to thine own self be true."[3] It is good advice for all of us, of course, especially in matters of vocation, because genuine callings are grounded in a sense of personal *authenticity*, in the God's honest truth of who we are. The call to authenticity is about *knowing* ourselves and *being* ourselves. It is about discovering, living, and *doing* the truth. In the words of Daniel Berrigan, it has to do with "living as though the truth were true."

In this chapter I want to explore some dimensions of the psychology and spirituality of vocational self-discovery, the process of learning who we are and what we have to offer to our world. There is an inherent tension in this process of

striving for wholeness and holiness, a need to find a discerning balance between *being* ourselves and *behaving* ourselves.
We are also faced with the complex challenge of achieving an
honest integration of personal authenticity and social responsibility. We do not discover ourselves in isolation, but only
within the complex web of relationships and forces that make
up the social context of the world in which we live. Justice
requires courageous attention to both individual and collective truth, a discerning awareness of our personal inner truth
and a critical consciousness of the larger, collective realities of
social sin and social suffering in our world.

TRUE SELF, FALSE SELF

The notion of an essential self calling from within for recognition and expression has a long, rich history in psychology
and in the ancient spiritual traditions of the world.

From a spiritual perspective, our true self is given or *revealed* to us by God. Our task, our calling, is to discover who
we are so that we can live our lives in such a way that we become the people we are truly meant to be. "For me," wrote
Merton, "to be a saint is to be myself. Therefore the problem
of sanctity and salvation is in fact the problem of finding out
who I am and of discovering my true self."[4]

Parallels are found in a number of psychological traditions. D. W. Winnicott, an influential British psychoanalyst,
developed his own theory of the "true self."[5] In *The Varieties
of Religious Experience*, the great American psychologist
William James called it the "wider self." "The conscious person is continuous with a wider self," he wrote, "through
which saving experiences come."[6] In his view, it is possible
for us to experience the saving, transformative power of the
sacred by living in tune with the rhythms and inclinations of

what has variously been called our deeper, truer, higher, or wider self.

The big question is "Who am I?" or "Who is the real me?" In my experience, one of the most useful criteria to consider in vocational discernment is whether we experience a *felt sense of authenticity* in relation to any particular life choice or direction we are considering or pursuing. In certain situations or activities, or with certain people, we experience a felt connection to our own personal truth, to our "real self" or "true self." In a letter to his wife, William James tried to describe the sense of integrity, vitality, and wholeness that accompanies such experiences:

> I have often thought that the best way to define a person's character would be to seek out the particular mental or moral attitude in which, when it came upon them, they felt most deeply and intensely active and alive. At such moments there is a voice inside which speaks and says "This is the real me!"[7]

Such experiences of authenticity can serve as important touchstones or reference points in our efforts to discern whether the paths we are considering are consistent with who we really are, with the "real me." In contrast are the times when we experience a jarring sense of inauthenticity or inner dissonance—a disconnect from the "real me." In such moments, it is as if we catch ourselves in the act of trying to be someone we're *not*. "Every one of us," says Merton, "is shadowed by an illusory person: a false self."[8] Instead of the sense of health and vitality that mark the presence of our true self, we experience a sense of emptiness and unreality that signals the presence of a "false self." Some lines from the Irish poet John Boyle O'Reilly capture the quality of such moments:

> I am sick of the showy seeming
> Of a life that is half a lie;
> Of the faces that are lined with scheming
> In the throng that hurries by.[9]

We feel sick or *get* sick on some level of our being when our life is based too much on "showy seeming" or "scheming" or pretense, when we get caught up in ways of living that are at odds with who we really are.

D. W. Winnicott's psychological theory may help to clarify some other aspects of the felt sense of authenticity that is an indicator of the presence of the true self.[10] He made a distinction between the true self and the false self (or the "false self on a conformity basis").[11] The true self, according to Winnicott, is rooted in the experience of the primary, undistorted, spontaneous, moment-to-moment unfolding of our own inner emotional reality. The true self is grounded in our personal emotional truth, our true feelings, what we actually think and feel about things. It is rooted in the emotional reality of what *is,* rather than in what we think we *should* be feeling. Our true feelings are what William Lynch has called our "psychological facts," whether or not we like them, express them, or even admit them to ourselves or others.[12]

The false self, on the other hand, develops during childhood out of fears that one's actual emotional reality is unacceptable, out of concerns that one's parents or family or culture cannot or will not tolerate or accept who one actually is. It feels emotionally *dangerous* to be oneself. Consequently, in order to cope and survive emotionally, the person develops a kind of inauthentic mask that is motivated by the need to adjust or conform to the expectations and wishes of others, either to win their approval or to avoid their rejection. The mask, to which Winnicott refers as the false self, serves both to conceal and to protect the true self, which remains hidden, and, in extreme cases, even forgotten or repressed within the unconscious of the person. This defensive, fear-driven way of being inevitably gives rise to marked feelings of inauthenticity, self-alienation, and disconnection from inner emotional reality.

The search for the true self (or the recovery of a connection with it that has been lost) necessarily involves efforts to remember what one's true feelings once were, or to recognize and feel what they are right now. Such efforts are often at the heart of the painstaking and painful process of psychotherapy for people who never had the feeling that it was safe or permissible to actually be themselves.[13] In the context of the emotionally secure, growth-promoting environment of the psychotherapeutic relationship, it is sometimes possible for people to come to know what it feels like to actually be themselves for the first time. Harry Guntrip writes:

> I cannot think of psychotherapy as a technique but only as the provision of the possibility of a genuine, reliable, understanding, and caring personal relationship in which a human being whose true self has been crushed by the manipulative techniques of those who only wanted to make her "not be a nuisance" to them, can begin to at last feel her own true feelings, and think her own spontaneous thoughts, and find herself to be real.[14]

Most people do not experience this degree of pathological self-alienation. Many of us, however, can fairly easily resonate with the distinction between fear-driven inclinations toward conformity versus freer inclinations toward authenticity. On an emotional level, the task for discernment centers around differentiating emotional truth from emotional falsehood, recognizing the difference between authentic and counterfeit ways of being in the world. Our emotional and spiritual health are put at risk when our self-protective and self-concealing inclinations begin to interfere with our emotional and relational development.

In my clinical experience, some of the most painful and complicated dilemmas having to do with authenticity are experienced by people who do not easily fit in with our culture's definitions of what is "normal" or "beautiful." For example, one dimension of the reality of who we are is our sexual orientation. Because of prevailing prejudices about homosexuality in church and society, many gay and lesbian people struggle with feelings of shame and self-hatred that make it more difficult for them to accept themselves for who they are, to make peace with the God-given fact of their own homosexuality.[15] Physical appearance is another aspect of who we are. Because of an excessive focus on external appearances in our culture, many girls and women whose bodies do not conform to whatever body type is currently fashionable struggle with painful doubts about whether they are loved and lovable as they are—in the body that God gave them.[16]

A final issue relevant to the call to authenticity centers around the tension between following the example of others versus discovering our own unique path. The unfolding of our vocation can be profoundly influenced by people whose lives have served as models or inspirations for us. These might include important mentors from our personal history as well as heroes from the history of humanity. Ultimately, however, we are not called to imitate the patterns of holiness that others have provided for us, however noble and beautiful these may be. Rather, we are called to discover our own pattern, our unique personal path to holiness. Jung suggests that this applies even to the imitation of Christ:

Are we to understand the "imitation of Christ" in the
sense that we should copy his life...or in the deeper
sense that we are to live our own proper lives as truly
as he lived his in all its implications? It is no easy
matter to live a life that is modeled on Christ's, but it
is unspeakably harder to live one's own life as truly as
Christ lived his.[17]

In the same spirit, Martin Buber tells an old Jewish story
about a rabbi named Zusya who once had a profound insight into what authenticity is all about: "In the world to
come," says Rabbi Zusya, "I shall not be asked 'Why were
you not Moses?' Instead, I shall be asked: 'Why were you not
Zusya?'"[18]

WHOLENESS AND HOLINESS

In the call to authenticity there is an inherent tension in our
strivings for wholeness and holiness. The tension centers
around the complex moral task of finding a discerning balance between *being* ourselves and *behaving* ourselves.

Holiness and wholeness have different associations in the
minds of most people. They seem to be organized around different principles, oriented toward different aims, motivated by
different values and ideals. *Holiness* is usually associated with
our aspirations toward *moral perfection* or *self-transcendence*. It has
to do with rising above our human weaknesses and limitations
so that we can live up to certain standards of righteousness
and good behavior. From this perspective, holiness requires efforts to tame or conquer our unruly, disordered, sinful selves,
which might otherwise incline us in unholy directions if we
are not careful to keep them in check and focused in the right
direction. *Wholeness*, on the other hand, is associated with

strivings for *integration* or *completion* or *self-realization*. Instead of focusing on overcoming the self, the emphasis is on embracing or accepting or expressing ourselves in all our complexity and imperfection. In a nutshell, wholeness is about *being* ourselves and holiness is about *behaving* ourselves.[19]

We are called to both wholeness and holiness. Although they have different emphases, it is possible for these seemingly contradictory aims to work together in harmonious and complementary ways. Perhaps the most complex moral challenge we face in our discernment of these simultaneous calls is the problem of what to do with all of the aspects of ourselves that don't neatly fit with our ideal mental image of the person we think we should be, our idea of what a "good" or "holy" person is like. In psychoanalysis, this is referred to as our *ego ideal*. For example, if our ego ideal centers around the idea that we should always and everywhere be loving and compassionate, we are likely to experience considerable discomfort when we experience feelings and inclinations in ourselves that do not seem particularly "nice" or loving or compassionate.

The *shadow* was Jung's name for all of the dimensions or parts of ourselves that do not conform to our ego ideal. The word *shadow* does not necessarily mean that these aspects of ourselves are bad or sinful, but rather suggests that some dimensions of our inner experience are darker or morally ambiguous and may not comfortably fit with the kind of self we aspire to be in the light of day. In my clinical practice I have worked with many idealistic, conscientious people over the years (especially those from Christian backgrounds) whose shadow side is often associated with thoughts and feelings related to anger, sex, and personal emotional needs. For example, feelings of anger that are perfectly appropriate in certain situations make some people extremely anxious and guilty, usually because anger conflicts with their idea of what it means to be a loving person. Natural sexual feelings and desires can also create inner conflict and tension because they are perceived as self-centered or sinful. In a similar way, normal human needs for attention and love from others may be perceived as "selfish" because they do not seem to be sufficiently generous and other-centered.

The shadow is perceived as emotionally, spiritually, and morally dangerous for good reasons. If we act out our shadow side thoughtlessly or irresponsibly, we are likely to get ourselves into all kinds of unhealthiness and trouble. Anger that is not carefully sorted out and expressed properly can be hurtful to others and damaging to our relationships. Irresponsible acting out of sexual feelings, of course, can also have disastrous consequences for ourselves and others. Likewise, an excessive and unbalanced focus on gratification of our own needs is a manifestation not only of egocentrism but also of a poorly developed conscience. And so a discerning attitude, common sense, and self-restraint are called for in all of our dealings with the shadow side of ourselves.

On the other hand, the seemingly dark and destructive feelings and inclinations associated with the shadow can also potentially play an important and constructive role in our personal growth and development. While impulsive action has its dangers, problems also develop when we get caught up in the opposite problem of *denying* or *repressing* the shadow side of ourselves. Defensive denial of our own inner reality reflects a lack of psychological honesty. When it is based on pretense and denial, being a "good person" can also mean acting as a kind of false self. If we are too defensive, too controlled, *too good* all the time, we lose touch with our authentic feelings and all of the vital life energies they contain. When we are out of touch with our anger and our sexual passions, our capacity for authentic emotional and spiritual passion can become blocked.

Unconsciousness of our shadow also makes us more prone to hypocrisy and judgmental attitudes toward other people. If we are unable to admit our weaknesses to ourselves, we are more likely to project them onto others. We end up criticizing in others what we are actually ashamed of and afraid to look at in ourselves. There is great psychological wisdom in Jesus' teachings about these matters:

> Why do you see the speck in your neighbor's eye but do not notice the log in your own eye? Or how can you say to your neighbor, "Friend, let me take out the speck in your eye," when you yourself do not see the log in your own eye? You hypocrite, first take the log out of your own eye, and then you will see clearly to take the speck out of your neighbor's eye.[20]

And so the call to authenticity requires psychological honesty, which means that we need to acknowledge and take responsibility for the shadow dimensions of ourselves. When we do this, we are able to judge ourselves and others with more accuracy and fairness. Just because something makes us uncomfortable does not mean that it is bad. From God's perspective, things might look very different.

The challenge centers around finding the proper attitude to take toward our shadow, the right kind of discerning consciousness with which to regard our inner experience. In psychoanalysis, this complex attitude or state of consciousness has been referred to as "conscious, loving self-restraint."[21] The basic ingredients of conscious, loving self-restraint are psychological honesty and a commitment to loving care and respect for ourselves and others. We must be courageously honest in acknowledging our own inner truth, including shadow feelings and inclinations that may seem very hateful and objectionable, while also being very conscientious and responsible about our attitude and behavior with others.

In the Zen Buddhist tradition, something comparable to "conscious, loving self-restraint" is summed up by the term "mindfulness." The essence of this attitude or state of consciousness is a relaxed, compassionate, nonjudgmental awareness of whatever we may happen to be experiencing at any given moment. This includes our experiences of events and people in the external world as well as the thoughts and feelings that enter into our awareness within the internal world of our own mind. Thich Nhat Hanh, a Vietnamese Zen master, refers to this kind of compassionate, loving awareness of our own inner emotional experience as "mindfulness of the mind." He gives some very practical, gentle advice on how to handle unwelcome thoughts and feelings that may not fit with our conscious program or plans:

> To take hold of your mind, you must practice mindfulness of the mind. You must know how to observe and recognize the presence of every feeling and thought which arises in you.... When a feeling or thought arises... the intention isn't to chase it away, hate it, worry about it, or be frightened by it. So what exactly should you be doing with such thoughts and feelings? Simply acknowledge their presence.[22]

The great emotional and spiritual challenge of the call to wholeness is learning to acknowledge and accept and love ourselves as we are. "Loving oneself is no easy matter," says James Hillman, "just because it means loving all of oneself, including the shadow where one is inferior and socially so unacceptable."[23] This humbling awareness of our own weaknesses helps us to be less judgmental and more forgiving toward other imperfect human beings. Paradoxically, the capacity to love and care for our imperfect selves is exactly what enables us to develop a more mature and generous love for others. The calls to wholeness and holiness come together in a right love for ourselves that frees us to be more just and compassionate in our dealings with others.

TRUTH AND LIES, WAR AND PEACE

"I vow to seek the truth, to live by the truth, and to confront untruth wherever I find it," was a solemn vow taken by Gandhi and his followers.[24] Authenticity as a guiding principle for living applies to more than just the way in which we conduct our personal lives. It also applies to the ways in which nations and peoples conduct themselves in the world. And so there are both individual and collective dimensions to truth and falsehood.

One way to gauge our dedication to the truth is to examine the integrity and sincerity of our individual and collective efforts to resolve differences and conflicts with others in an honest and peaceful manner without resorting to violence. Do we cultivate an attitude of "conscious, loving self-restraint" in our personal dealings with other persons and in our collective dealings with the governments and peoples of other nations? In Gandhi's view, truth goes hand in hand with nonviolence, just as untruth goes with violence. "The way of peace is the way of truth," he wrote. "Truthfulness is even more important than peacefulness. Indeed, lying is the mother of violence."[25] From a psychological perspective, M. Scott Peck offers a similar insight: "Lying is simultaneously one of the symptoms and one of the causes of evil, one of the blossoms and one of the roots."[26]

"Matters of state and the heart that start with a lie," wrote Maureen Dowd, "rarely end well."[27] In matters of state, the practice of deception—especially when the aim is to justify the resort to needless violence—is not only a violation of the public trust but also a gross violation of the human rights of all those who are caught up in the crossfire of the resulting war. Sadly, there is widespread concern and considerable evidence that two of America's most controversial wars have been initiated and carried out under false pretenses. This was the case for the Vietnam War, and it is now the case for the ongoing war in Iraq. In Mark Twain's story "The Mysterious Stranger," written in 1910, the tragic link between lies and war is described in a way that sounds eerily familiar almost a hundred years later:

> The loud little handful—as usual—will shout for the war. The pulpit will—warily and cautiously—object—at first; the great, big, dull bulk of the nation will rub its sleepy eyes and try to make out why there should be a war, and will say, earnestly and indignantly, "It is unjust and dishonorable, and there is no necessity for it." Then the handful will shout louder.... Next the statesmen will invent cheap lies, putting the blame upon the nation that is attacked, and every man will be glad of those conscience-soothing falsities, and will diligently study them, and refuse to examine any refutations of them; and thus he will by and by convince himself that the war is just, and will thank God for the better sleep he enjoys after this process of grotesque self-deception.[28]

Certain kinds of "conscience-soothing falsities," especially when they are repeated often enough by the media in the form of disinformation, can have the effect of dulling or blunting our consciences, causing us to lose our ability to distinguish between what is true and what is not. We end up being lulled into a kind of "deceit-induced stupor."[29] "The repetition of falsehoods tied to the war on terrorism and the war against Iraq," says James Carroll, "has eroded the American capacity, if not to tell the difference between what is true and what is a lie, then to think the difference matters much."[30] Unfortunately, this seems to have been a widespread problem during the buildup to the Iraq War. We see it in the shifting rationales for the necessity of the war, and in the pattern of new justifications for it being advanced as each of the previous ones are recognized as false (no weapons of mass destruction, dubious connections between Iraq and Al Qaeda and 9/11, the illusion that war will reduce the risk of terrorism at home, the hypocrisy and impossibility of promoting democracy through military occupation of another country).

To "hear the word of reality" we must make an effort to be *accurately informed* about reality. This is especially important given our recent history, as it is now widely recognized that an uncritical mainstream U.S. media became caught up in a government propaganda and disinformation campaign to drum up public support for the project in Iraq by manipulating people's fears about weapons of mass destruction and terrorism in the aftermath of 9/11. We must bring a discerning, critical consciousness to bear in evaluating the information we get from our government through the media. To ensure that we get the straight story, we should, whenever possible, do a "fact check" by seeking out alternative sources of news and information. We should also do an interior emotional and spiritual "fact check" to assess whether the information we get from the government and media "rings true" for us.

Words can be misused to cover up the truth, to distort reality, to make things look different from what they actually are, to conceal or minimize embarrassing facts. "Words alter, words add, words subtract," wrote Susan Sontag in an essay titled "Regarding the Torture of Others," which was published during the period of widespread public shame and shock after the photos of tormented Iraqi prisoners at Abu Ghraib had appeared on the cover of every newspaper.[31] Sontag noted

how senior government officials were careful to avoid use of
the word *torture,* preferring instead more benign-sounding
words like *abuse* or *humiliation.* "My impression is that what
has been charged thus far is abuse," said the secretary of defense, "which I believe is technically different from torture.
...And therefore I'm not going to address the 'torture' word."[32]
The refusal to address the "torture" word is a refusal to address
the awful truth. It also trivializes the appropriate human response to the reality revealed in the photos: *shame.* The words
of the prophet Jeremiah are fitting:

> To whom shall I speak and give warning, that they
> may hear? See, their ears are closed, they cannot listen.
> ...They have treated the wound of my people care-
> lessly, saying, "Peace, peace" when there is no peace.
> They acted shamefully, they committed abomination,
> yet they were not ashamed. They did not know how
> to blush.[33]

Persons of conscience must "know how to blush" and have a
capacity to feel shame when it is appropriate to be ashamed.
Such feelings are indicators that our conscience is in working
order, that we have a heart, that we are *human.* "The quickest
way to lose your humanity," says William Sloane Coffin, "is to
begin to tolerate the intolerable."[34]

To "hear the word of reality" we must listen, first of all, to
the reality of the victims of war. We must "treat the wound of
God's people carefully." It is much easier to forget the victims,
for the simple reason that it is unpleasant to think about them.
In the case of Iraq, we must begin with the horrifying reality
of all the innocent Iraqi people who have been killed and in-
jured and traumatized because of our invasion and occupation
of their country. As I write, the most well-researched, conser-
vative estimate is that a minimum of twenty-five thousand

Iraqi civilians have died violent deaths as a result of the war.[35] The traumatic shock and grief of their loved ones and families and all those who witnessed these deaths are unimaginable. There is also the disturbing phenomenon of the kind of desperation and rage that seems to be motivating increasing numbers of people to become suicide bombers.

We must also remember the soldiers who are being misused and abused in a questionable cause, whose lives are being put on the line in an impossibly stressful, no-win situation. As I write, more than two thousand have been killed and more than fifteen thousand have been seriously wounded in Iraq. There are also the harder to quantify, hidden injuries to minds and spirits that result from constant exposure to traumatic violence, from participating in or witnessing atrocities in what psychiatrist Robert Jay Lifton has called an "atrocity-producing situation."[36] A recent popular song, written with American soldiers in mind, poignantly captures the high-stakes consequences of choices made in moments of extreme ambiguity and stress at checkpoints in Iraq, when split-second decisions must be made about whether an approaching car is another nervous Iraqi civilian or a deadly suicide bomber bent on destruction:

> We've got God on our side,
> And we're just trying to survive.
> What if what you do to survive
> Kills the things you love?
> Fear's a powerful thing,
> It'll turn your heart black, you can trust.
> It'll take your God-filled soul
> And fill it with devils and dust.[37]

The prisoners or "detainees" who are being held in U.S. military facilities in places like Abu Ghraib in Iraq, Bagram

Air Force Base in Afghanistan, and Guantanamo Bay, Cuba, must also not be forgotten. By designating prisoners as "unlawful combatants," our government has officially taken the position that certain people are not entitled to basic human rights guaranteed by U.S. and international law, and can therefore be imprisoned for indefinite periods of time without charges or trial. Worse, there is mounting evidence that many such prisoners are systematically subjected to cruel torture and maltreatment during interrogation.[38]

Finally, there are all the unseen victims who are killed indirectly by the war. These are all of the men, women, and children in Iraq and elsewhere who are being killed slowly through neglect and disease and hunger because precious funds and resources that *could* be used for constructive, life-enhancing, life-saving purposes are being diverted into the destructive project in Iraq. Above all else, we must remember the impact of war on the most vulnerable. "We must keep the painful truth of the victims before us," says Dean Brackley, "because...the victim offers us the privileged place...to encounter the truth that sets us free."[39]

THE TRUTH WILL MAKE YOU FREE

"You will know the truth," said Jesus, "and the truth will make you free."[40] Knowledge of the truth alone, however, is not enough to set us free. We must also sense the moral implications of the truths we discover for how we live our lives—and do our best to live our lives in accord with them. In the words of Enda McDonagh, we must "do the truth."[41] Michael Himes adds another ingredient, *love,* saying that we are called to "do the truth in love."[42] Connors and McCormick make the connection between truth and conscience in our efforts not only to discern but to *do* the right thing:

It is our conscience which enables us to "do the truth," not just to seek it out and find the morally right option, but to choose it as well. For the mature and well-developed consciences of good persons give evidence of their moral character, integrity and wisdom, express their hunger for goodness and truth, reveal their skills at moral reflection and discernment, and empower them to seek out and embrace the good which must be done.[43]

There is a kind of luminous sense of truth and integrity about certain "good persons" that can become a source of nurturance and inspiration for the rest of us in our efforts to seek and know and do the truth. Dorothy Day, the founder of the Catholic Worker Movement, who is well-known for her radical commitment to nonviolence, social justice, and service to the poor, is a notable example of a person who "did the truth" over the long haul. In his introduction to her autobiography, *The Long Loneliness,* Daniel Berrigan says of her:

I am grateful beyond words for the grace of this woman's life, for her sensible, unflinching rightness of mind, her long and lonely truth, her journey to the heart of things. I think of her as one who simply helped us, in a time of self-inflicted blindness, to see.... She urged our consciences off the beaten track. ... She did this, first of all, by living as though the truth were true.[44]

It is not hard to think of recent examples of other wonderful people who "lived as though the truth were true." Some, like Bishop Juan Gerardi of Guatemala, have paid a heavy price for sticking up for God's truth. After peace accords were agreed upon between the Guatemalan government and a coalition of guerrilla groups in 1996 to end a horrifically cruel civil war that lasted over three decades and claimed over two hundred thousand lives, the Catholic Church in Guatemala carried out a unique pastoral initiative known as the "Recovery of Historical Memory" project (better known by its initials as REHMI). Bishop Gerardi, the coordinator of the Human Rights Office of the Archdiocese of Guatemala, presided over the project, which basically involved seeking out and telling the truth from the standpoint of the victims of Guatemala's civil war, most of whom were impoverished indigenous Mayan people from the highland areas of the country. The great majority of human rights violations (including more than fifty thousand people who were "disappeared," shocking massacres of innocent civilians, thousands of extrajudicial executions, and systematic use of sadistic torture) were carried out by Guatemalan military and paramilitary forces. Thousands of heartbreaking personal testimonies and stories of victims and witnesses of human rights violations were carefully and sensitively collected from around the country and eventually documented in a lengthy, four-volume report. The "wound of God's people" was treated with great care and respect.

On April 24, 1998, Bishop Gerardi publicly released the REHMI report with a speech marking the occasion at the Metropolitan Cathedral in Guatemala City. "The essential objective behind the REHMI project," he said, ". . . has been to know the truth that will make us all free." He went on:

> *Truth* is the primary word, the serious and mature action that makes it possible for us to break this cycle of death and violence and to open ourselves to a future of hope and light for all. REHMI's work has been an astonishing endeavor of discovery, exploration, and appropriation of our personal and collective history. It

has been an open door for people to breathe and speak in freedom and for the creation of communities with hope. Peace is possible—a peace born from the truth that comes from each one of us and from all of us. It is a painful truth, full of memories of the country's deep and bloody wounds. It is a liberating and humanizing truth that makes it possible for men and women to come to terms with themselves and their life stories. It is a truth that challenges each one of us to recognize our individual and collective responsibility and to commit ourselves to action so that those abominable acts never happen again.[45]

Two days after speaking these words, Bishop Gerardi was beaten to death in his garage by a team of military assassins to silence and punish him for his interest in the truth—and to scare others who might wish to follow his example.

Gerardi's words, of course, do not apply only to the uniquely tragic situation in Guatemala. They resonate deeply with all of us, everywhere. And, in spite of his sad end, there is something mysteriously consoling and inspiring about Bishop Gerardi's beautiful words and his courageous example. On a recent visit to Guatemala, I noticed interesting graffiti spray-painted on the wall of the Metropolitan Cathedral where he gave his last speech: *"Gerardi Vive!"* ("Gerardi Lives!"). I was reminded of some lines from the poet James Russell Lowell that were often quoted by Dr. Martin Luther King Jr.:

> Truth forever on the scaffold,
> Wrong forever on the throne
> Yet that scaffold sways the future
> And, behind the dim unknown
> Standeth God within the shadow
> Keeping watch above his own.[46]

5

PASSION AND COMPASSION
The Heart's Calling

For where your treasure is, there will your heart be also.
—Matthew 6:21

OUR SENSE OF VOCATION is intimately linked to the people and things that move us to passion and compassion. We cannot answer the authenticity question, "Who am I?" without also answering the passion question, "What do I really want?"[1] We discover who we are only by becoming conscious of the most authentic desires, loves, and longings of our hearts. "Who am I?" is also closely related to another question, "*Whose* am I?"[2] We come to know ourselves by recognizing those to whom we *belong*. Whom do we love? With whom do we feel at home? To whom does our heart go out? With whose sufferings and aspirations do we most identify?

In this chapter I want to explore some of these reasons of the heart that shape and influence our callings. The experience of falling in love, for example, is sometimes associated with a profound sense of vocation. There is also the issue of the complex interrelationship between our own desires and God's desires. Finally, I will discuss ways in which the stirrings of compassion in our own hearts can put us in touch with the heart of God.

REASONS OF THE HEART

In vocational discernment, it is important to pay close attention to our feelings, because authentic callings always begin with a stirring of the heart. Someone or something moves or touches us in some way, and our heart responds with a *feeling*. We may not, at first, be able to articulate or make sense of our heart's response; we know only that something significant has occurred on the affective level of our experience. "The heart has its reasons," wrote Pascal, "that reason does not know."[3]

There is no general "one-size-fits-all" answer to the very personal question of what we should do with our lives. We must consult our hearts, asking ourselves the question: "Is my *heart* in this path?" This is the point of a story told by the great Jewish philosopher Martin Buber:

> Rabbi Baer of Radoshitz once said to his teacher the "Seer" of Ludlin: "Show me one general way to the service of God." The zaddik [a wise and holy person] replied: "It is impossible to tell people what way they should take. For one way to serve God is through learning, another through prayer, another through fasting, and still another through eating. Everyone should carefully observe what way their heart draws them to, and then choose this way with all their strength."[4]

The story is titled "The Particular Way." Each of us must find our own particular way by carefully observing our feelings about the options before us. Where, or to what, or to whom, are we drawn?

An authentic calling should *feel* right. As has been discussed, an important criterion to consider in vocational discernment is the degree of emotional or intuitive "rightness" we experience as we consider or pursue any particular path or direction. Intuition is itself a kind of inner voice that sometimes gives us useful information and guidance from within. We might, for example, experience an uneasy feeling that a particular career move, or a relationship with a certain person, is simply *not* right for us. We may not be able to explain it or justify it; we just *know* it. On the other hand, in a moment of blessed clarity, we might experience an intuition that a particular course of action or relationship *is* just right for us, a sense that things are "meant to be."

"To be meant," says James Hillman, "implies a transcendent power that calls, chooses, or means something with one, a power that gives meaning."[5] Joseph Campbell's famous advice to "follow your bliss" in matters of vocation assumes that we have within ourselves an intuitive capacity to recognize the kinds of things that give us personal joy and meaning—and the kinds of things that *don't*. "We are having experiences all the time," says Campbell, "which may on occasion render...a little intuition of where your bliss is. Grab it. No one can tell you what it is going to be. You have to learn to recognize your own depth."[6]

Learning to recognize our own depth requires that we become comfortable and at home with the affective, nonrational dimension of ourselves. Conscious awareness of our inner emotional experience helps us to be more receptive and attuned to the messages of our inmost self or conscience, which tends to speak in a language that is different from the linear, logical process of our rational mind or consciousness. "In order to be in touch with the conscience-coordinating calls of the Self, a new skill has to be acquired by rational consciousness," writes Edward Whitmont. "It has to learn to receive and decipher the urges and warnings of the Self which arise from the nonrational, hitherto unconscious sources."[7] The challenge is to make the unconscious conscious, to allow the reasons of the heart a voice in our conscious, rational decision-making and discernment. This allows us to develop perspective and insight into our feelings and desires before acting on them. "It is when the reasons of the heart become known to the mind...that insight occurs," says John Dunne.[8]

Therefore, there is a kind of emotional intelligence that we can bring to bear in important decisions about the direction of our lives. Vocational discernment, however, is not just a simple matter of trusting our hearts, because intuitions and feelings are sometimes wrong. Consulting our hearts is crucial, but there is also a place for our "heads" in this process. "Discernment and decision-making demand a balanced perspective," writes Michael O'Sullivan. "Put simply, it is all right to trust our feelings as long as we use our heads."[9]

FALLING IN LOVE

The experience of falling in love is often accompanied by a profound sense of vocation. The awakening of romantic love or sexual passion for another person is perhaps the most common manifestation of this powerful experience, but it is actually just one among many different forms of falling in love. It is possible, for example, to fall in love with a field of study or work, with a way of living, with an idea or a place. Our hearts can also be captured or captivated by a movement, or a people, or by God. The experience of falling in love is an expression of our heart's capacity for deep passion and feeling for someone or something other than ourselves.

The powerful feelings of romantic and sexual passion that are released within us when we fall in love with another person hold the promise of deep joy and fulfillment. They can also lead to great grief, hurt, disillusionment, and disappointment. Our hearts can draw us into relationships that have the potential to evolve into mature, committed love with someone who is a perfect match for us, but can also lure us into troubled, unhealthy entanglements that are all wrong. A discerning attitude and common sense are essential when we are under the influence of powerful romantic and sexual passions. We are wise to trust our feelings but use our heads in approaching these complex, high-stakes matters of the heart.

Because of its potential to get us into so much trouble, the perfectly natural and beautiful experience of falling in love is sometimes seen as a lesser form of love, an immature form of infatuation based in childish fantasy. It might, for example, make us prone to projecting unrealistic "god" or "goddess" qualities onto the object of our love, a projection that can distort or obscure that person's actual, imperfect reality as a human being. Though all of this is sometimes true, it is important not to diminish or disparage the powerful experience of falling in love. Regardless of how things turn out with the actual person, the experience evokes deep, slumbering passions in us that provide precious emotional and spiritual opportunities to know ourselves on a deeper level.

People in love often experience a heightened sense of spiritual aliveness and perception. This is the experience of young Stephen Dedalus, the main character in James Joyce's novel *A Portrait of the Artist as a Young Man*. A famous passage describes the ecstatic spiritual awakening Stephen experiences one day after meeting the eyes of a young Irish lass by the seashore:

> Her image had passed into his soul for ever and no word had broken the holy silence of his ecstasy. Her eyes had called him and his soul had leaped at the call. To live, to err, to fall, to triumph, to recreate life

out of life! A wild angel had appeared to him, the
angel of mortal youth and beauty, an envoy from the
fair courts of life, to throw open before him in an in-
stant of ecstasy the gates of all the ways of error and
glory. On and on and on and on![10]

In his memoir *The Sacred Journey*, Frederick Buechner
poignantly describes a similar personal experience that occurred when he was an emotionally vulnerable teenage boy a
few years after the tragic suicide of his father:

> She was a girl going on thirteen as I was, with a
> mouth that turned up at the corners. If we ever spoke
> to each other about anything of consequence, I have
> long since forgotten it.... But one day at dusk we
> were sitting side by side on a crumbling stone wall
> watching the Salt Kettle ferries come and go, when
> ... our knees happened to touch for a moment, and
> in that moment I was filled with such a sweet panic
> and anguish of longing for I had no idea what. I
> knew my life could never be complete until I found
> it.... It was the upward-reaching and fathomlessly
> hungering, heart-breaking love for the beauty of the
> world at its most beautiful, and, beyond that, for that
> beauty east of the sun and west of the moon which is
> past the reach of all but our most desperate desiring
> and is finally the beauty of Beauty itself, of Being it-
> self and what lies at the heart of Being.[11]

Buechner's experience could, of course, be reduced to
the awakenings of adolescent sexuality that are inflated and
spiritualized in the mind of a naïve young boy. Though there
may be some truth to such an unromantic Freudian interpretation, from a deeper spiritual perspective it misses the

whole point, which is the "sweet panic and anguish of long-ing for I had no idea what" and the recognition that "I knew my life could never be complete until I found it." The point is to figure out what the longing is for, and to do whatever we need to do to find the thing that will make our life complete.

There are other forms of falling in love. The capacity to fall in love begins very early. Interestingly, research in early childhood development has shown that, ideally, the relation-ship between parents and very young infants is a kind of mu-tual falling in love. Loving, playful interaction between parents and babies is seen as nurturing and promoting many aspects of physical, cognitive, emotional, and even moral develop-ment, including brain growth, muscle and motor coordi-nation, problem-solving and reasoning skills, emotional security, self-esteem, and capacities for emotional give-and-take and empathy that are the foundation for all future rela-tionships. A passage from Dr. Stanley Greenspan, a respected child psychiatrist and specialist in early childhood develop-ment, conveys some of the complexity and richness of these early interactions:

> When your baby flashes you a joyful smile, she's con-veying a whole wealth of information about herself to you. As she melts you with her grin, she's not just passively radiating her love for you. She wants to see you so much that she's shifting her body and learning to use her muscles to better focus on you. She's also turning to the sound of your voice because she is ex-cited by your voice and wants to see where the sound is coming from. Your baby displays her yearn-ing for you in the way she strains to prop herself on her forearms, or rolls over to get a better look at you, or eventually tries to remain sitting without falling.

She is driven to practice these new physical mile-
stones because she has taken a passionate interest in
you and the world you introduce to her.[12]

Taking a passionate interest in others and the world
around us is what falling in love is all about. Ultimately, such
passions vibrate with the passion and love of God. This is
the gist of the well-known saying attributed to Father Pedro
Arrupe:

Nothing is more practical than finding God, that is,
than falling in love in a quite absolute, final way. What
you are in love with, what seizes your imagination,
will affect everything. It will decide what will get you
out of bed in the morning, what you will do with
your evenings, how you will spend your weekends,
what you read, who you know, what breaks your
heart, and what amazes you with joy and gratitude.
Fall in love, stay in love and it will decide everything.[13]

OUR DESIRES AND GOD'S DESIRES

Vocational self-discovery is closely bound up with discovering what we really want. The secret of vocation, according to
Michael Himes, is to "discover what it is you most truly and
deeply want when you are most really and truly you." Holy
desires that orient us in the direction of our true calling originate in our true self or "best self." "When you are at your
best," Himes asks, "what is it that you most truly desire?"[14]

Although the scriptures remind us that "God is greater
than our hearts," there is a way in which God uses the desires
of our hearts to lead us to our destiny.[15] From a spiritual perspective, it is possible to see our own deepest and most au-

thentic desires as God's desires *in* us or *for* us. James Fowler puts it well: "What God wants for us and from us has something central to do with what we most deeply and truly want for ourselves."[16] There is a mysterious connection, it seems, between the will of God and our own heart's desire.

In an essay on the central place of "great" or "holy" desires in the spirituality of Saint Ignatius Loyola, E. Edward Kinerk observes that some of our desires seem to orient us more reliably toward God than others.[17] Careful consideration and evaluation of the depth, authenticity, and generosity of our desires are at the heart of discernment in the Ignatian spiritual tradition, which basically centers around the task of making subtle differentiations between different kinds of desires. The challenge lies in recognizing the difference between the superficial, inauthentic, self-centered desires of the ego and the deep, authentic, loving desires of the inmost self. The basic idea is that the latter are more likely to be in line with our true calling, with God's purpose or will or design for our lives. In a nutshell, if our desires are leading us in the direction of increasing superficiality, phoniness, or selfishness, we are probably on the wrong track. If, on the other hand, our desires are inclining us in the direction of increased personal depth, authenticity, and generosity, we can be fairly sure that we are on the right track.

The strength or intensity of our desires is also an important consideration. In some religious circles, passionate desires are regarded as morally or spiritually dangerous. This reflects a confusion between the intensity of desire and the object of desire, a blurring of the distinction between ego-centered and God-centered desires. An undiscerning, unreflective pursuit of egocentric desires can, of course, be disastrous both for ourselves and others. In the matter of desires, we must always be responsible and "use our heads." On the other hand, weak or insufficient spiritual desire is also hazardous to our moral and spiritual health. A too-cautious approach to desire, a fear of desiring too much, can have a constricting and deadening effect on our spiritual lives. In his essay "The Weight of Glory," C. S. Lewis argued that the greatest peril lies not in desires that are too strong but in desires that are too *weak*:

> Indeed, if we consider the unblushing promises of reward and the staggering nature of the rewards promised in the Gospels, it would seem that our Lord finds our desires, not too strong, but too weak. We are half-hearted creatures, fooling around with drink and sex and ambition when infinite joy is offered us.... We are far too easily pleased.[18]

The problem with desiring too little is that we are more prone to end up settling for *less* than what we really want in important vocational matters of love and work. To use the words of an old Irish ballad, one day we look at the life we have chosen for ourselves and realize: "It isn't gold, sure 'tis brass I find!" Instead of being "on fire" with desire, we are lukewarm, tepid, half-hearted, "far too easily pleased." A story from the early Desert Fathers captures the distinction in an interchange between a cautious young monk and a wise older monk who invites him to a much bolder way of being in the world:

> Abbot Lot came to Abbot Joseph and said: Father, according as I am able, I keep my little rule, and my little fast, my prayer, my meditation and contemplative silence; and according as I am able I strive to cleanse my heart of thoughts: now what more should I do? The elder rose up in reply and stretched out his hands to heaven, and his fingers became like ten lamps of fire. He said: Why not be changed totally into fire?[19]

In a similar spirit, but from a very different vantage point, the legendary performer Josephine Baker once asked: "Is that what they call a vocation, what you do with joy as if you had fire in your heart, the devil in your body?"[20] The way of vocation has been called "the way of the burning heart."[21] The gospel story of the disciples on the road to Emmaus suggests that a "burning heart" may be one of the signs of genuine encounter with the Risen Christ: "Were not our hearts burning within us," the disciples asked each other, "while he was talking to us on the road?"[22]

Finally, it is important to remember that the way of the burning heart is ultimately not just about "me" and my personal fulfillment but about "us" and the common good. Kinerk makes the point that the deepest and most authentic desires of the human heart are "public":

> Authentic desires are always in some way public. This is a paradox, for certainly our desires reflect what is most uniquely personal in ourselves, but at the same time the more deeply we go into ourselves the more these uniquely personal desires manifest a communal reference point instead of an individual one. Superficial desires—such as those linked to consumerism—demonstrate all too graphically our cultural narcissism, but more authentic desires always lead us out of ourselves and into the human community. When desires to feed the hungry, to clothe the naked, and to use our gifts for the service of others become more compelling than private concerns, we will know that we have matured spiritually.[23]

Cesar Chavez is a beautiful example of a person who was motivated by "public" desires. A Mexican American who became the leader of the United Farm Workers Union, Chavez spent many years working tirelessly and selflessly for the rights of poor and exploited migrant farm workers in the United States. Once, when asked about what motivated him to keep doing such work on behalf of others, he responded:

> What keeps me going? Well, it's like a fire—a consuming, nagging, every day and every-moment demand of my soul to just do it. It's difficult to explain. I like to think it's the good Spirit asking me to do it. I hope so.... If you really want something, you have to sacrifice. Because of my faith the concept of sacrifice is understood.[24]

COMPASSION AND THE HEART OF GOD

Compassion is a particular kind of passion that has been defined as "the deep feeling of sharing the suffering of another, together with the inclination to give aid or support or to show mercy."[25] The Latin roots of the word mean "to suffer with." One of the ways callings come to us is through the compassionate stirrings of our own hearts. There is a mysterious way in which compassion puts us in touch with the heart of God.

The best description I have come across of what compassion actually *feels* like is from Black Elk, the Lakota Sioux holy man. Telling the story of the first time he was called upon to heal a sick person (a little boy from his community who had fallen deathly ill), he described the unusual feeling that came over him as he prayed for the recovery of the little boy:

> ...I cried to the Spirit of the World, and while I was doing this I could feel the power coming into me

from my feet up, and I knew that I could help the
sick little boy. I kept on sending a voice, while I made
low thunder on the drum, saying "My Grandfather,
Great Spirit . . . the two-leggeds on earth are in despair. For them, Grandfather, I send a voice to you. . . ."
While I was singing this I could feel something queer
all through my body, something that made me want
to cry for all unhappy things, and there were tears on
my face.[26]

Although Black Elk does not directly link his feeling of
"wanting to cry for all unhappy things" with the healing
power he felt coming into him "from his feet up," they are
clearly connected. The healing powers of love and compassion have long been recognized in the religious traditions of
the world. The compassionate Jesus, of course, is the best-
known healer in the history of the world. Special note is
made in many of the gospel healing stories of Jesus' heart response to the people who sought his help:

A leper came to him begging him, and kneeling he
said to him, "If you choose, you can make me clean."
Moved with pity, Jesus stretched out his hand and
touched him, and said to him, "I do choose. Be made
clean!"[27]

"Moved with pity" is variously translated in other versions as
"moved with compassion" or "feeling sorry for him." However it is labeled, the core experience is a heart response to
the sufferer accompanied by an "I do choose" inclination to
do something to relieve that person's pain.

The word *compassion* is rarely used in modern psychology, but its psychological parallel, *empathy,* is widely recognized as an essential ingredient in psychological healing.

Empathy is the capacity to feel or imagine ourselves into the world of another person in order to vicariously know something of what it is like to be in that person's situation, to develop a feeling for what he or she is feeling. The ability to empathically listen—and then to communicate our empathic understanding to the other person in such a way that the person feels heard or understood—is at the core the process of psychotherapy and of all genuine connection and understanding between human beings. The "talking cure" originally developed by Sigmund Freud is now associated with a diverse range of sophisticated theoretical principles and therapeutic techniques, but none of them are effective if they are not built upon a foundation of empathic feeling and understanding. In an unguarded moment, Freud himself once wrote in a letter to Jung: "Essentially, one might say the cure is effected through love."[28]

Beyond the one-to-one connection, there are collective dimensions to empathy and compassion. Sometimes we have a special feeling for whole peoples or communities. Because of our unique personal backgrounds and histories, our hearts may be particularly responsive to certain kinds of people or problems. Universal compassion for all humanity is a worthy ideal, but on a practical level most people are more likely to personally identify with the sufferings or aspirations of certain groups of people (e.g., children with special needs, oppressed minorities, victims of hunger or war). Sometimes very specific vocations grow out of a feeling of "suffering with" particular groups of others. Compassion and our sense of social justice are related in the sense that compassion helps us to appreciate how certain unjust conditions, policies, and ideologies hurt and deprive particular groups of people in particular ways.

The opposite of compassion is *indifference,* which is a kind of emotional or spiritual numbness characterized by an inability to be touched or moved by the needs and sufferings of others, accompanied by a sense of apathy regarding the unjust or hurtful conditions that cause the hurt or deprivation in the first place. The awakening of compassion involves a change of heart, a personal transformation, a movement from a numb, unfeeling, self-centered perspective to a deepened capacity for heartfelt compassion and just behavior. In the words of the prophet Ezekiel, "I will remove the heart of stone from their flesh and give them a heart of flesh," says the Lord.[29] Our "heart of flesh," our natural heart, feels and responds like the heart of God. It beats with the heartbeat of God.

There are connections between grief, compassion, and justice. In *The Prophetic Imagination*, Walter Brueggemann proposes that the function of the prophet is more than just to criticize the unjust status quo. Rather, the prophet is called to give voice to God's grief and pain and anguish over how badly things are going for God's people.[30] In a similar spirit, Cornel West says that the language of prophecy is the language of "cries and tears":

> Divine compassion undergirds the divine love of justice just as human compassion undergirds the prophetic love of justice. The premier prophetic language is the language of cries and tears because human hurt and misery give rise to visions of justice and deeds of compassion. . . . [Compassion] awakens us from fashionable ways of being indifferent to other people's suffering or from subtle ways of remaining numb to the social misery in our midst.[31]

The prophet articulates the heartache and heartbreak of God for the poor and the oppressed, for the "least" and the "last" of this world. Some verses from Jeremiah give a glimpse into the soul of the heartbroken, grief-stricken prophet who hurts with those who are hurting the most:

For the hurt of my poor people I am hurt,
I mourn, and dismay has taken hold of me.
Is there no balm in Gilead?
Is there no physician there?
Why then has the health of my poor people not been
        restored?
O that my head were a spring of water,
And my eyes a fountain of tears,
So that I might weep day and night
for the slain of my poor people![32]

The vocational question, it seems, has to do with identifying *those for whom we hurt*. To which of God's people do our hearts seem to go out to most? Whose sufferings and aspirations are speaking or calling to us? *Where*, or *to whom*, does our heart seem to be leading us?

"To whom does my heart belong?" is another way to put the question. A stark and beautiful illustration of how a creative answer to this question was worked out in one life can be found in the story of Father Stanley Rother, an American priest whose heart mysteriously led him all the way from the plains of his native Oklahoma to a Mayan community at the base of a spectacular volcano in the highlands of Guatemala.[33] A simple man, not a particularly good student and not viewed as an especially promising leader, Rother eventually found his niche as the pastor of a church serving the Tzutuhil Mayan people of the town of Santiago Atitlan.

Over the fourteen years during which he lived in Santiago Atitlan, Rother's humility, quiet kindness, and generosity earned him great respect and affection from the poverty-stricken people of that beautiful place. He was not a political man, yet his loving commitment to the people during a period of mounting violence and political repression was nonetheless interpreted as "subversive" by government and military authorities. "To shake the hand of an Indian," said Rother, "is a political act." It was only a matter of time before Rother himself, like so many of those he served, would also fall victim to the repression. On the night of July 28, 1981, he was murdered by a death squad in his room at the church rectory.

When parishioners heard what had happened to their beloved pastor, hundreds of grief-stricken and outraged people filled the plaza in front of the church and refused to be dispersed. Over the next few days, as arrangements were being worked out to send his body back to Oklahoma to be buried, it became apparent that the local people were reluctant to allow Rother's body to be taken away. They felt that he belonged with *them* and made known the fact that they wanted him to be buried *there*. Eventually, an unusually creative compromise was worked out between his family and the people of the town: Rother's *heart* would be removed from his body. His body would be returned to Oklahoma, but the people of Santiago Atitlan would be allowed to keep his heart. It is still buried there in a place of honor in the church of Santiago.

In her poem "The Gringo's Heart," Renny Golden portrays the final negotiations, in which a Mayan catechist is mediating between the local people and representatives of the family back in Oklahoma:

"We'll make arrangements,
fly the body to Oklahoma, to his parents."

A cofradia leader moves forward,
behind him centuries of silence,
held, like a breath, like a heart stopped.
"No," he says,
"The priest belongs to us."

For days there are phone calls, entreaties.
When I rise to speak, our leaders listen
because I knew you best.

"Keep his heart," I say,
"send Stanley back to Oklahoma."
Through a translator I ask your mother's permission.
When she cries, I add, "The heart that broke for
        us."[34]

6

VISION
The Quest for a Worthy Dream

Where there is no vision, the people perish.
— Proverbs 29:18 (King James Bible)

For a dreamer lives forever, and a toiler dies in a day.
— John Boyle O'Reilly, "The Cry of the Dreamer"[1]

"THE HEARING EAR AND THE SEEING EYE," reads the Book of Proverbs, "the Lord has made them both." Although the root metaphor for vocation centers around the "hearing ear," finding and following our callings also requires a "seeing eye," a capacity for perception and vision and imagination. This might, for some, involve actual visionary experiences of another level of reality, mystical glimpses into the world of the spirit. More commonly, it has to do with seeing the reality of this world more clearly, looking more deeply into things, beneath the surface of things. It might have to do with seeing the sacred in the ordinary, intuiting the hidden potential in ourselves and others, sensing possibilities and envisioning alternatives in what otherwise looks like an impossible or hopeless situation.

This chapter addresses some of the connections between vocation and our capacity for vision and imagination. I will begin by discussing a traditional Native American ritual known as the vision quest to see what it can teach us about seeking a guiding vision for our lives. I will also explore the potential in the dreams we have each night to help us in discerning our callings. This will be followed by an examination of what developmental psychologists call "the Dream," which has to do with our capacity to imagine or envision a meaningful future for ourselves. Finally, we will consider the call each one of us has to develop our capacity for prophetic imagination, to find our own way of making the Dream of God a reality in our world.

THE VISION QUEST

Among the Native American cultures of the great plains of the western United States, it was common for members of the community to undertake a strenuous ritual known as the vision quest in an effort to seek a guiding vision or dream for their lives.[2] This ritual was practiced by the indigenous peoples of North America for centuries, and is still practiced by some Native Americans today.

Although the vision quest was usually undertaken by boys and men, visions were also sought by girls and women. The vision-seeker would approach the shaman, a wise and holy member of the community experienced in such matters, to discuss his or her particular need or purpose for seeking a vision, and for assistance with the ritual process of carrying out the quest. It was important to select an appropriate place, usually a rugged, remote, lonely hilltop or butte away from the distractions of community life, to seek and wait and pray for the vision. A sweat lodge ceremony was undertaken for purposes of spiritual purification and preparation prior to going off alone to the vision-questing place, where the seeker would remain alone to fast and pray, usually for at least one full day and night, sometimes for as long as two, three, or even four days and nights. After the quest, the seeker reviewed the entire experience with the shaman so as not to miss any of its meanings or implications for his or her life.

During the vision quest, the seeker was instructed to pray earnestly and humbly for guidance and direction from Wakan Tanka (the Lakota Sioux name for God, which translates into English as the "Great Mystery" or "Great Mysteriousness"). The seeker was urged to pay careful, scrupulous attention to everything that he or she experienced during the vision quest so as not to miss any possible messages or help that might be forthcoming from God. Messages might come through external events in the natural world as well as through the inner world of personal consciousness. For example, the attentive and alert vision-seeker might discern important meanings in the appearances of particular animals or birds, or in changes in the weather. Messages might also come in the form of spiritual insights, through the imagery of actual visions while the seeker was awake, or in the form of dreams during sleep.

In the Lakota language, the word for the vision quest ritual is *hanblecheya*, which translates into English as "crying for a vision" or "lamenting for a dream." The "crying" or "lamenting" suggests that visions do not come easily. The vision must be *earned* by a humble person with a sincere heart through the ordeal of fasting and suffering. The seeker must recognize his or her need for help and direction and guidance from a power beyond the self. Reaching out across religious traditions in words that challenge many of the assumptions of current American culture about the nature of "reality," John Lame Deer, another Sioux holy man, says we must "thirst for a dream from above":

Crying for a vision, that's the beginning of all religion. The thirst for a dream from above, without this you are nothing. This I believe. It is like the prophets in your bible, like Jesus fasting in the desert, getting his visions. It's like our Sioux vision quest, the *hanblecheya*. White men have forgotten this. God no longer speaks to them from a burning bush. If he did, they wouldn't believe it, and call it science fiction. Your old prophets went into the desert crying for a dream and the desert gave it to them. But the white people of today have made a desert within themselves. The White Man's desert is a place without dreams or life. There nothing grows. But the spirit water is always way down there to make the desert green again.[3]

The vision quest ritual, however, has value as more than just an illustration of the deep appreciation for the symbolic imagery of dream and vision in Native American spirituality, from which modern Western people have much to learn. The vision quest also embodies a harmonious integration of the personal spiritual quest with service to the community, of personal vocation with social conscience. The vision is sought not just for oneself, but for the benefit of the group. It helps the seeker to find a place in the community, to discern his or her unique way of contributing to the common good:

> The nature of a vision quest is spiritual, it is a search for meaning and direction. In the Lakota tradition, the vision sought is not for individual self-fulfillment alone. Rather the search is for the individual to find his or her unique contribution to the community; a vision quest occurs in a communal context.[4]

A poignant example is found in the life of the Native American healer and social activist Leonard Crow Dog, who lives on the Rosebud Sioux reservation in South Dakota. During his own vision quest, Crow Dog had the following visionary experience, which revealed not only *what* his calling was to be, but for *whom* it was meant:

> Suddenly, before me stretched a coal-black cloud with lightning coming out of it. The cloud spread and spread; it grew wings; it became an eagle. The eagle talked to me: "I give you a power, not to use for yourself, but for your people. It does not belong to you. It belongs to the *ikche wichasha*, the common folks."[5]

Crow Dog's vision offers an important reminder that seeking a vision for our life is ultimately not only about us, but about finding a way to make the world a better place for the "common folks."

DREAMS: GOD'S FORGOTTEN LANGUAGE

Dreams and visions are similar in that both involve a flow of symbolic imagery through our consciousness before our mind's eye. The basic difference is that we experience visions when we are awake and dreams while we are asleep. Visions are also much less common, especially in modern European-American culture. Dreams, on the other hand, are very common; contemporary research suggests that *everyone* dreams every night, even if they are unable to remember their dreams upon awakening.

The idea that dreams sometimes convey important messages to us from a source of wisdom deep within or beyond ourselves is found not only in modern psychology but also in many ancient spiritual traditions of the world. "A dream not understood," goes the saying in the Jewish Talmud, "is like a letter not opened." Sadly, as John Lame Deer lamented, appreciation for the symbolic language of dreams has been largely forgotten in our culture, and so these nightly "letters" remain unopened, their messages undeciphered, their meanings not understood or taken to heart in the way we live our lives. Because of their neglected spiritual potential, dreams have been referred to as "God's forgotten language."[6]

Native American vision-seekers were instructed to pay careful attention to any dreams they might have during periods of sleep on their vision quest. The idea was that God might use dreams as a way to convey messages or to answer their prayers for guidance. This is what Black Elk had to say about dreams:

> Even though we sleep we are still close to Wakan Tanka, and it is very often during sleep that the most powerful visions come to us; they are not merely dreams, for they are much more real and do not come from ourselves, but from Wakan Tanka.[7]

A similar belief that God might use dreams as a way to speak to human beings is also found in the Hebrew and Christian scriptures. "It seems strange how much there is in the Bible about dreams," wrote Abraham Lincoln. "If we believe the Bible, we must accept the fact that, in the old days, God and his angels came to [people] in their sleep and made themselves known in dreams."[8] There are many examples: "Hear my words," reads the Book of Numbers, "when there are prophets among you, I the LORD make myself known to them in vision, I speak to them in dreams."[9] In the book of Job we find these striking passages about dreams and nightmares:

> Now a word came stealing to me,
> my ear received the whisper of it.
> Amid thoughts from visions of the night,
> when deep sleep falls upon mortals.

Dread came upon me, and trembling,
which made all my bones shake.
A spirit glided past my face;
the hair of my flesh bristled.
It stood still,
but I could not discern its appearance.
A form was before my eyes;
there was silence, then I heard a voice:
Can mortals be righteous before God?
Can human beings be pure before their Maker?

For God speaks in one way,
and in two, though people do not perceive it.
In a dream, in a vision of the night,
when deep sleep falls on mortals,
while they slumber on their beds,
then he opens their ears,
and terrifies them with warnings.[10]

The idea that God, or angels as messengers of God, might visit or speak to human beings in dreams is also encountered in the New Testament. For example, no less than five dreams are recounted in the story of the birth of Jesus in Matthew's gospel. When Joseph is scandalized that Mary, his wife-to-be, is pregnant by someone else before their marriage, we are told that an angel of the Lord appeared to him in a dream and said, "Joseph, son of David, do not be afraid to take Mary as your wife, for the child conceived in her is from the Holy Spirit." Later, the wise men are also warned through a dream about King Herod's evil intentions, and Joseph has three other dreams that warn and guide him so that he can protect the infant Jesus and keep him safe from harm.[11]

There is a fascinating passage from the Book of Daniel that displays remarkable psychological wisdom and insight into the meaning and purpose of dreams. As the story goes, Daniel, a

Hebrew prophet who was also a gifted dream interpreter in ancient Babylon, was summoned by King Nebuchadnezzar to interpret one of the king's dreams. The specifics of the story and the dream are less important than Daniel's explanation of the purpose of dreams to the king: "This mystery has not been revealed to me because of any wisdom that I have more than any other living being, but in order that the interpretation may be known to the king and *that you may understand the thoughts of your mind.*"[12] The New King James Bible translation is "... *that you may know the thoughts of your heart.*" The purpose of dreams, then, according to Daniel, is to help us know the thoughts of our own mind or heart; understanding our dreams helps us to *know ourselves.*

The idea that the symbolic imagery of dreams is meaningful and that interpretation of dreams can yield rich insight into ourselves was the foundation of Freud's classic work *The Interpretation of Dreams,* which, after its publication in 1900, established him as a towering figure in modern psychology. Freud saw dream images as symbolic portrayals of what is going on in our unconscious mind at any given time. Jung, one of Freud's early disciples, who later had a falling out with him over differences in their views of dreams, the unconscious, and religion, was in basic agreement with Freud that dreams are a valuable resource for self-knowledge and insight into our inner depths. Freud, however, tended to see the unconscious as a repository of emotions and memories that are unacceptable to our conscious mind, while Jung saw the unconscious as having great spiritual potential, as being a rich source of guidance and wisdom within ourselves.

Jung made a distinction between our conscious ego (our everyday identity) and our unconscious inner Self, which he saw as a source of spiritual wisdom that *sends* or *gives* us dreams as a way to help and guide us in living our lives. One of the ways dreams do this is by revealing ourselves *to* ourselves—in the sense that our unconscious, inner self is revealed to our conscious ego through the symbolic imagery of our dreams. Our dreams help us to know the thoughts of our own mind or heart by making what is unconscious *conscious*.

Jung's idea that dreams are a form of communication from a source deep within ourselves, from Someone or Something beyond or other than our own ego, strikingly parallels the ancient spiritual view of dreams as a potential means for God to guide and help us. The psychological task for our ego is to learn to listen to dreams for the voice of our unconscious inner self; the spiritual task is to learn to listen for God. A passage from John Sanford integrates and summarizes both views of dreams:

> Suppose someone told you that there was something that spoke to you every night, that always presented you with a truth about your life and soul, that was tailor-made to your individual needs and particular life-story, and that offered to guide you throughout your lifetime and connect you with a source of wisdom beyond yourself. And, furthermore, suppose all of this was absolutely free. Naturally you would be astonished that something like this existed. Yet this is exactly the way it is with dreams.[13]

The complexities of the art and skill of dream interpretation are beyond the scope of this book. Suffice it to say that dreams use symbolic or metaphorical language that is foreign and unfamiliar to our usually logical, rational ways of thinking, and that learning to understand our dreams is like learning a new language. Like learning any foreign language, learning to work with our dreams takes time, patience, and practice. Dreamwork is also something that is best done with the help of a trustworthy therapist or spiritual director who has some familiarity and experience with dreams.

Learning to work with our dreams, like learning to pray, begins with *listening*. The correct attitude is exemplified in the biblical story of young Samuel. Perplexed and confused by a voice that he hears calling him whenever he falls asleep in the temple, Samuel tells Eli, a wise older person, about what is happening to him. Eli gives Samuel some advice that all of us could take to heart:

> Then Eli perceived that the Lord was calling the boy. Therefore Eli said to Samuel, "Go, lie down; and if he calls you, you shall say, 'Speak, Lord, for your servant is listening.'"[14]

THE DREAM WITH A CAPITAL "D"

In *Walden,* the journal of his experiment with living a simple, contemplative life in the woods around Walden Pond, Henry David Thoreau wrote:

> I learned this, at least, by my experiment, that if one advances confidently in the direction of his dreams and endeavors to live the life which he has imagined, he will meet with a success unexpected in common hours.[15]

By "dreams" it is clear that Thoreau is not thinking of the kind we have at night when we are asleep. Rather, he is referring to our capacity for envisioning or imagining a meaningful future for ourselves, a kind of image in our mind's eye of our fondest personal hopes and aspirations. Developmental psychologists, and the theologians who apply their insights to faith development, call this the *Dream*:

> The Dream, with a capital D, is something more than night dreams, casual daydreams, pure fantasy, or a fully

designed plan. This Dream has a quality of vision. It is
an imagined possibility that orients meaning, purpose,
and aspiration. The formation of a worthy Dream is
the critical task of young adult faith.[16]

The concept of the Dream was first developed by psychologist Daniel Levinson in *The Seasons of a Man's Life.*[17] He saw
the challenge of defining a personal Dream as a crucial developmental task of young adulthood. James Fowler has
summarized Levinson's thinking on the Dream as "the formation in young adulthood of a vision of the self, projected
into the future, that gives a young person the energy, the
sense of destiny and direction, and the courage to move pur-
posefully into the ambiguities and difficulties of adult life."[18]
Early efforts to test out the Dream ("endeavors to live the
life which we have imagined") are also a necessary part of
the process of refining and "fine-tuning" our Dream through
the ups-and-downs of real life.

From a spiritual perspective, the Dream is not something
we invent through our own creative or clever imaginings.
Rather, it is a gift that is *given* to us by God, just as visions
were given to earnest young Native American seekers on
lonely hilltops. In keeping with the visual metaphor, the
Dream is *revealed* or *shown* to us in our mind's eye as a kind of
guiding image for our life. Although the root metaphor for
vocation centers around *hearing* calls, there is a way in which
the Dream enables us to *see* our call by envisioning a way of
living, loving, and working that reflects our most cherished
ideals and values. In *Big Questions, Worthy Dreams,* Sharon
Daloz Parks makes the spiritual connection between Dream
and vocation:

> The Dream understood through the eyes of the great
> traditions of faith across time is more than imagining
> a job or career or profession narrowly understood.

The Dream in its fullest and most spiritual sense is a sense of vocation. Vocation conveys calling and meaningful purpose. It is a relational sensibility in which I recognize that what I do with my time, talents, and treasure is most meaningfully conceived not as a matter of mere personal passion or preference but in relationship to the whole of life. Vocation arises from a deepening understanding of both self and world, which gives rise to moments of power when self and purpose become aligned with eternity.[19]

Some Dreams embody more than just a personal vision for our own future. They look beyond the personal self to the greater good of the world around us. They not only point to our own hidden potential for personal growth and self-realization but also allow us to discern the latent, unseen possibilities for transformation in our world. Daloz Parks writes:

> Images of self that encourage high aspiration and excellence in meaningful terms (in contrast to mere success) enable the young adult to see beyond self and world as they presently are and to discern a vision of the potential of life: the *world as it ought to be* and the *self as it might become.*[20]

PROPHETIC IMAGINATION
AND THE DREAM OF GOD

Some people have unusually big and generous dreams of "the world as it ought to be." They possess a kind of prophetic imagination that enables them to look beyond the world as it is to the world as it *could* be or *should* be.[21] Their personal dreams embody something of God's Dream for the world. Each of us, in our own way, is called to cultivate our capacity for prophetic imagination, to find our own way of making the Dream of God a reality.

Borrowing the phrase from Verna Dozier, Marcus Borg develops the concept of the "Dream of God" in his book *The God We Never Knew*.[22] In a broad sense, the Bible is the story of the Dream of God expressed in many different images and voices through the often nightmarish course of human history. God dreams of a world where "justice rolls down like waters," where "swords are beaten into plowshares," where people "act justly, love tenderly, and walk humbly." The Dream, in a nutshell, is "a social and political vision of a world of justice and peace in which human beings do not hurt or destroy, oppress or exploit one another."[23] In the Hebrew scriptures, it was embodied in all the rich associations of the word *shalom*:

> The dream of God is a vision of *shalom,* which translates as "peace" but meaning much more than the absence of war. It means well-being in a comprehensive sense. It includes freedom from negatives such as oppression, anxiety, and fear, as well as the presence of positives such as health, prosperity, security. *Shalom* thus includes a social vision: the dream of a world in which such well-being belongs to everybody.[24]

"The dream of God blazed forth again in Jesus," says Borg.[25] It is evident in Jesus' radical social vision, his special fondness for the poor and the oppressed, his inclusive "politics of compassion." God's Dream can be discerned in Jesus' own mission to "bring good news to the poor...release to the captives...recovery of sight to the blind...and to let the oppressed go free."[26] It is perhaps most clearly embodied in one of his most frequently used phrases: "the kingdom of God." Although there is an other-worldly dimension to this mysterious term, it is clear that, for Jesus, the "kingdom" was also very much a this-worldly phenomenon, something to be individually and collectively worked for so that it can be realized as much as humanly possible during our lives in this world: "Thy kingdom come, thy will be done, on earth as it is in heaven." The kingdom is a dream of the world as God would have it be.

In *The Prophetic Imagination,* Walter Brueggemann argues that prophetic vision does not originate in dreamy fantasies of how the world could someday be a better place. Rather, he says, it begins by taking a hard, realistic look at the condition of things as they actually are right now. It begins with "imagining the real." Forming a worthy dream, according to Daloz Parks, "depends upon serious engagement with the truth of the world, the universe as it is, including 'things that should not be so.'"[27] It depends upon access to "fitting, vital images" of both the heights and the depths of the human condition. Such images may be based on first-hand experiences or personal observations; they may also come by way of literature or film or news of the world in which we live. They can include glimpses of the sufferings and horrors of the world as well as sightings of the wonder and beauty of God's creation in spite of it all.

The images that sustain and motivate people of vision are not always positive. The fascinating, interview-based research of Daloz Parks and her colleagues suggests that, for some, haunting images of "what should not be so" are the most compelling:

> When asked for images that sustained them, a surprising number of people spoke, not of dreams of justice, but of specific injustices and examples of cruelty and suffering that they had seen. These images seemed to serve as powerful icons for what should not be so.[28]

Brueggemann argues that the primary calling of the prophet is not to be an angry social critic, but rather to be someone who, first of all, is willing to take an honest look at upsetting and unsettling realities that are denied or ignored by society at large and the powers-that-be. The tragic consequence of such denial is widespread public "numbness" and moral complacency about things that would otherwise evoke grief and outrage.[29] A sad current example is the way the American government and media carefully screen, control, and "spin" the flow of information and images of the Iraq War. An "out of sight, out of mind" policy has applied not only to mounting American casualties, but even more to the terrible suffering the war has caused for the Iraqi people. Bob Herbert writes:

> The vast amount of suffering and death endured by civilians as a result of the U.S.-led invasion of Iraq has, for the most part, been carefully kept out of the consciousness of the average American.... You can't put a positive spin on dead children. As for the press, it has better things to cover than the suffering of civilians in war.... There's been hardly any media interest in the unrelieved agony of tens of thousands of innocent civilians in Iraq. It's an ugly subject, and the idea has taken hold that Americans need to be protected from stories or images of the war that might be disturbing. As a nation we can wage war, but we don't want the public to be too upset about it.... Out of sight, out of mind.[30]

On a psychological level, prophetic consciousness requires a willingness to allow into our awareness unsettling truths about "what should not be so" that we might be tempted to pretend are not there. This sometimes means *looking* at things we would prefer not to look at and *feeling* things we would prefer not to feel. The prophet is then called to help others to do likewise. Brueggemann describes three dimensions of the task of the prophet in a "numbed" social situation:

> 1. To *offer symbols* that are adequate to confront the horror and massiveness of the experience that evokes numbness and requires denial...

> 2. To *bring to public expression those very fears and terrors* that have been denied so long and suppressed so deeply that we do not know they are there...

> 3. To *speak metaphorically but concretely about the real deathliness that hovers over us and gnaws within us,* and to speak neither in rage nor with cheap grace, but with the candor born of anguish and passion.[31]

The great African American poet Langston Hughes offers a beautiful example of the kind of prophetic thinking and speech that Brueggemann is talking about. Lamenting the sad fact of so much wasted human potential in the inner city, Hughes used the metaphor of "deferred dreams" to ask hard questions about the heavy personal and social costs of poverty and racism in American society:

> What happens to a dream deferred? Does it dry up
>   like a raisin in the sun?
> Or fester like a sore—and then run?
> Does it stink like rotten meat?
> Or crust and sugar over—like a syrupy sweet?
> Maybe it just sags like a heavy load.
> Or does it explode?[32]

Deferred dreams of individuals are sad enough, but there is also a way in which the collective dreams of whole peoples can be deferred, crushed—even killed off. In a heartbreaking passage from *Black Elk Speaks,* the Lakota holy man recalls what went through his mind as he surveyed the grim aftermath of the massacre of hundreds of unarmed Sioux by the U.S. Cavalry at Wounded Knee Creek in winter 1891:

> And so it was all over. I did not know then how much was ended. When I look back now from this high hill of my old age, I can still see the butchered women and children lying heaped and scattered all along the crooked gulch as plain as when I saw them with eyes still young. And I can see that something else died there in the bloody mud, and was buried in the blizzard. A people's dream died there. It was a beautiful dream.[33]

Entire peoples whose lives and dreams are at stake have been referred to as the "crucified peoples" of the world. This was the jarring phrase used by Father Ignacio Ellacuría, one of the six Jesuits murdered (along with their housekeeper and her daughter) at the University of Central America in El Salvador on November 16, 1989. Jon Sobrino, a member of the same Jesuit community whose life happened to be spared because he was away at the time of the murders, has written with great anguish and passion of crucified peoples:

> The first thing we discovered in El Salvador was that this world is one gigantic cross for millions of people who die at the hands of executioners. Father Ellacuría referred to them as "entire crucified peoples." And that is the salient fact of our world—quantitatively, because it encompasses two-thirds of humanity, and qualitatively, because it is the most cruel and scandalous of realities.... From this basic reality of the cross and of death, we have learned to place in its true perspective the massive poverty which draws

people to death—death which is slow at the hands of
the ever-present structures of injustice, and death which
is swift and violent when the poor seek to change
their lot.[34]

Sobrino goes on in a disconcerting way about the "most
cruel and scandalous" reality of the "crucified peoples" of our
world. For those of us who take for granted our status in the
world's privileged minority, he prophetically pushes the enve-
lope of our normal comfort zone. He means for the image
and the reality of "what should not be so" to provoke us, to
penetrate our numbness, to overcome our resistance, to push
us to examine our own unconscious complicities in—and responsibilities for—such a world:

> People do not want to acknowledge or face up to
> the reality of a crucified world, and even less do we
> want to ask ourselves what is our share of responsi-
> bility for such a world.... It isn't that we simply do
> not know; we do not *want* to know because, at least
> subconsciously, we sense that we have all had some-
> thing to do with bringing about such a crucified
> world.[35]

An honest look at "what should not be so" brings about
an acute awareness of how much the world as it is does not
reflect God's Dream of how it could be. It can also bring on a
depression. The overwhelming nature of the world's problems can evoke an immobilizing sense of hopelessness and
helplessness in us: hopelessness about the possibility that
things will ever change and helplessness to do anything about
it. It is at this point that we are especially in need of images of
hope to help us move from the depressing awareness of how
impossibly *bad* things are to a sense of realistic hope that "another way is possible."

In his book *Images of Hope: Imagination as Healer of the Hopeless,* William Lynch discusses the relationship between hope and imagination. Cautioning against notions of hope based on unrealistic utopian fantasies or impossible dreams, Lynch presents a modest, reality-based theory of hope as a *sense of the possible* in difficult situations:

> I define hope...as the fundamental knowledge and feeling that there is a way out of difficulty, that things can work out, that we as human persons can somehow manage internal and external reality, that there are "solutions" in the most ordinary...sense of the word. What we are saying is that hope is, in its most general terms, a sense of *the possible,* that what we really need is possible, though difficult, while hopelessness means to be ruled by the sense of the impossible.[36]

For Lynch, hope has to do with "imagining the possible" in any given difficult situation. A person suffering from severe depression, for example, may have to use considerable imagination to find a convincing reason to get out of bed in the morning. The poor must also draw upon the resources of imagination in their efforts to keep trying, versus giving up, in the face of discouraging adversity. In dealing with unjust social conditions or unjust wars, we must use our imagination and intuition to sense the hidden potentials and possibilities for what can be done in situations that otherwise appear to be futile or beyond hope. "Imagining the possible" can empower us by allowing us to see that it is possible to do *something* rather than nothing in a bad situation. "Possibility is the secret heart of reality," says Dan Hartnett. "There is nothing inevitable about an unjust situation; there are always new options available to us, however latent these may be."[37]

The gospel story of the "rich young man" offers some spiritual perspective on the matter of discerning what is possible or impossible in any given situation. After asking Jesus the question, "What must I do to inherit into eternal life?" the young man was "shocked and went away grieving" when Jesus suggested that he sell all his belongings and give the money to the poor. The disciples also seemed discouraged and confused by Jesus' rather shocking prescription, perhaps because it appeared to place unrealistic and even impossible demands on those who would follow him. "Then who can be saved?" they ask in dismay. "For mortals it is impossible," Jesus responds, "but not for God; for God all things are possible."[38]

7

SUFFERING
The Call of the Wounded Healer

In his poor heart man has places which do not yet exist and into them enters suffering in order to bring them to life.
—Leon Bloy, *Pilgrim of the Absolute*[1]

Here's the thing. . . . The thing I believe. God is inside you and inside everybody else. You come into the world with God. But only them that search inside for it find it. And sometimes it just manifest itself even if you not looking, or don't know what you looking for. Trouble do it for most folks, I think. Sorrow, Lord. Feeling like shit.
—Alice Walker, *The Color Purple*[2]

PAIN AND TROUBLE often play a mysterious role in the unfolding of our callings. Experiences of personal suffering, or encounters with the pain of others, offer spiritual opportunities that have the potential to put us in touch with the sacred dimension of experience from which callings emerge: "The LORD is near to the brokenhearted, and saves the crushed in spirit."[3] This being said, it is important not to romanticize or spiritualize suffering, to assume that it always has redemptive or transformative effects upon our consciousness or character. Pain can call forth the best in us, but it can also bring out the worst.

In this chapter I want to explore some dimensions of the complex relationship between suffering and vocation. There is a degree of pain that goes with the territory of any genuine calling. There is also a way in which certain life problems and symptoms themselves sometimes seem to have a way of conveying important messages to us about the direction of our lives. For some people, callings originate in painful life experiences that serve as a kind of initiation into the role of the "wounded healer." Many people in the helping and healing professions have had experiences of personal suffering that awakened in them a calling to compassionate service. At the heart of it all is the great mystery of redemptive suffering.

GROWING PAINS

"Life is difficult" is the first line of M. Scott Peck's popular and influential book *The Road Less Traveled*.[4] The "road" to which he is referring is the path of emotional and spiritual growth. The title implies that most of us prefer to take the easy way because the path to genuine growth and maturity can sometimes be so rough, so rugged, so difficult. It is not easy to change and grow, to honestly face our problems, to be loving and authentic persons in an egocentric, artificial culture.

Because of our egocentrism, all of us are inclined to *resist* the process of growth. Something in us doesn't *want* to change, and so we cling to the known and familiar rather than take the risk of following the Voice into the unknown. This is completely natural and understandable because there are no guarantees that we won't end up hurt or disappointed when we allow ourselves to be led into the new or the different. Sometimes the only way to a new heart is through a broken heart. Sometimes letting go of an old way of being so that something new can come into being is so painful it feels like *dying*. This, I think, is what Goethe is talking about in his poem "The Holy Longing":

> And so long as you haven't experienced this:
> To die and so to grow,
> You are only a troubled guest
> On the dark earth.[5]

The call to authentic personhood involves a commitment to continual growth and change, which requires a willingness to undergo the emotional and spiritual pain and discomfort that are a necessary and inevitable part of the process of coming to know ourselves. Self-protective, defensive efforts to avoid the pain of self-knowledge almost always end up bringing us other kinds of trouble. "Neurosis," says Jung, "is always a substitute for legitimate suffering."[6] The neurotic misery of an inauthentic existence, it seems, is the price we pay for refusing to embrace the pain and risk of living an authentic life. We end up living as "troubled guests" on the earth, spending our precious time and energy anxiously trying to escape from the risky business of becoming the persons we are meant to be.

The call to love also entails pain and risk. We experience growing pains with every step we take in the direction of becoming more loving persons, with every increase in our capacity to give and receive genuine love. Mature love requires that we find the energy and will to make the moral effort to extend ourselves on behalf of others—even when we don't feel like it. "I am sorry I can say nothing more consoling to you," says Father Zossima in *The Brothers Karamazov*, "for love in action is a harsh and dreadful thing compared with love in dreams."[7]

Learning to love is a difficult, humbling, life-long process for all of us. Rainer Maria Rilke offered this encouragement in a letter to a young poet wrestling with his callings in love and work:

To love is good, too: love being difficult. For one
human being to love another: that is perhaps the
most difficult of all our tasks, the ultimate, the last
test and proof, the work for which all other work is
but preparation. For this reason young people, who
are beginners in everything, cannot yet know love,
they have to learn it. With their whole being, with
all of their forces gathered closely about their lonely,
upward-beating heart, they must learn to love.[8]

SYMPTOMS AS A VOICE OF THE SOUL

We get sick in one way or another when we are living in a
way that is out-of-synch with who we really are. At such
times, the painful physical or emotional symptoms we experience can be interpreted as a wake-up call, as a kind of cry for
help from our soul.

In *Care of the Soul,* Thomas Moore suggests that the soul
sometimes uses painful or disruptive symptoms to get our attention, to convey a message to us from within when we are
falling into error or living in a way that is out-of-synch with
who we really are. From this perspective, the soul might
speak through a feeling of nagging anxiety, a knot in the
stomach, a stubborn depression we can't seem to shake, bore-
dom or burnout in our work, or a persistent inner sense of
spiritual restlessness or emptiness in spite of apparent contentment on the surface of our life. According to Abraham
Maslow, when our deeper spiritual needs are ignored or neglected, we get sick:

> If this essential core of the person is denied or sup-
> pressed, he [or she] gets sick, sometimes in obvious
> ways, sometimes in subtle ways.... This inner nature
> ... is weak and delicate and subtle and easily over-

come by habit, and cultural pressure. . . . Even though denied, it persists underground, forever pressing for actualization.[9]

Our first inclination may be to try to fix or cure the annoying or uncomfortable symptom, to rid ourselves of the thing that is disrupting the status quo of our life. We might, for example, try to talk ourselves out of the troublesome feelings, to deny or suppress them, to do whatever we can to make them go away. This is understandable, because no one wants to be in emotional discomfort or pain. From the perspective of the soul, however, this may be exactly the wrong approach, because it signals that we are unable or unwilling to hear what our soul may be trying to tell us through the symptom. If it is a cry for help from our soul, then the right thing to do is to pay attention. Instead of ignoring our own pain, we need to begin by compassionately listening to it, by allowing it to have a voice. James Hillman says it beautifully:

> The right reaction to a symptom may as well be a welcoming rather than laments and demands for remedies, for the symptom is the first herald of an awakening psyche which will not tolerate any more abuse. Through the symptom the psyche demands attention. Attention means attending to, tending, a certain tender care of, as well as waiting, pausing, listening. Precisely what each symptom needs is time and tender care and attention.[10]

Therefore, the best approach is to slow down, to try not to panic, to make an effort to listen patiently and carefully in order to learn what our painful feelings may be trying to teach us or tell us. "We should not try to 'get rid' of a neurosis," said Jung, "but rather to experience what it means, what it has to teach, what its purpose is. We should even learn to be thankful for it, otherwise we pass it by and miss the opportunity of getting to know ourselves as we really are."[11] In Jung's view, the neurotic symptom itself offers an opportunity or invitation to learn something about ourselves; it is a potential blessing in disguise.

Careful reflection on our symptoms not only can help us to diagnose what is wrong or missing in our life but can also give us clues as to what we need to do to get better. "The unconscious," says Sanford, "knows what we do not know and what we must learn about ourselves and life in order to become well."[12] Appreciating the meanings and getting the messages of our symptoms can teach us what our soul needs, what it may be craving or longing for. Is there something missing in our life, some need that we are neglecting? Is there some unfinished emotional or spiritual business that requires taking care of? Is there something we must do, some action we are called to take, that can help us to recover our emotional or spiritual health?

A few examples might help to illustrate this. A man whose life choices have been overly influenced by his concerns about financial security could begin to experience a nagging sense of emptiness or meaninglessness that money, possessions, status, or financial security do not take away. The feelings of emptiness or meaninglessness may be an invitation to take a hard look at what is missing in his life; they may be a kind of call to re-evaluate his priorities in light of the recognition that there is more to life than money. Or perhaps a woman's neurotic guilt and fear have always held her back by inhibiting her inclinations toward personal authenticity and individuation, with the result that she ends up feeling emotionally constricted and spiritually trapped by the circumstances she has chosen for herself. Her mounting desperation may signal the stirrings of a calling to overcome her fears by taking steps to liberate herself from her self-imposed bondage. Or maybe we have become depressed because our life has been so anxiously focused on conformity and pleasing others that we have forgotten who we really are. The depression itself may help us figure out what is wrong and what we need to do to live in a more authentic and satisfying way.

Finally, if we are willing to learn, symptoms can teach us *humility*. The spatial metaphor for where we are located emotionally or spiritually when we are sick or suffering is *down*. Spiritually, we find ourselves in the "valley of the shadow of death" or in the "belly of the whale." Emotionally, we are brought low by depression or disappointment or emotional trouble. We are reminded of our weakness, our vulnerability, our lack of control—including control over emotional states that cannot be overcome by the power of our own will:

> Symptoms humiliate; they relativize the ego. They bring it down. Cure of symptoms may but restore the ego to its former ruling position. The humiliation of symptoms is one of the ways we grow humble—the traditional mark of the soul.[13]

Such humbling and even humiliating experiences serve as a reality check for our ego. They remind us that we are not God, and they put us in touch with our need for a power greater than ourselves to heal and save us from whatever is ailing us.

THE WOUNDED HEALER

Sometimes callings originate in painful life experiences that serve as a kind of initiation into the way of the *wounded healer*—the person whose sufferings become a source of healing to others.

The vocational theme or pattern of the wounded healer can be discerned in many religious traditions through the ages. It is perhaps most dramatically illustrated in the spirituality and healing practices associated with shamanism, an ancient, primordial form of religion that is still practiced in many indigenous cultures today. Parallels to shamanism are found in many of the world's major religious traditions. The theme of the wounded healer can be detected in the life pattern of the historical Jesus as well as in the lives of many people in the contemporary world. Henri Nouwen's well-known book, *The Wounded Healer: Ministry in Contemporary Society*, is centered around the idea that the minister's own wounds, if tended properly, can become a source of healing for others.[14]

Although a great diversity of spiritual beliefs and healing practices exists among shamanistic cultures throughout the world, certain universal patterns are encountered wherever shamanism is practiced.[15] One of the most striking is the phenomenon of the "initiatory illness" in the calling of the shaman. In many cultures, it is common for the shaman-to-be to experience a painful physical illness or psychological crisis at some point during childhood, adolescence, or young adulthood. During the initiatory illness the young person typically has vivid visions and dreams (often while in a state of unconsciousness or delirium) that contain striking religious imagery centering around images of death and rebirth, spirit journeys, or encounters with various kinds of good and evil spirits associated with illness and healing. Black Elk, for example, received his calling through a complicated and remarkable vision during his own illness experience, which occurred when he was only nine years old and lasted over a period of twelve days while he was deathly ill in a coma-like state of unconsciousness.[16]

Eventually, the shaman recovers from the initiatory illness and begins a period of formal training and apprenticeship in preparation for healing work with others. Significantly, the illness experience is interpreted by the community as a sign that the young person has a special calling to the work of healing. After young Black Elk recovered from his own severe illness at the age of nine, an older shaman by the name of Whirlwind Chaser said to his parents: "Your boy is sitting there in a sacred manner. I do not know what it is, but there is something special for him to do."[17]

The shaman's later wisdom and power to heal others are attributed to the profoundly formative—and transformative —experience of his or her own initiatory illness. This personal experience of pain and illness, according to David Kinsley, is seen as one of the shaman's primary qualifications for helping and healing others:

> Healers become qualified to heal because they have experienced serious illness deeply and completely and have overcome it, survived it, learned from it, and been transformed by it. In dealing with people who are sick, shamans can help because they have experienced what the patient is suffering and have mastered it.[18]

There are many vivid accounts of initiatory illness experiences. Dorcas, a female shaman (*sangoma*) from southern Africa who was bed-ridden with a severe illness for three years, offered these thoughts on the initiatory illness:

> No one becomes a sangoma without first getting sick. Everyone who is called by the spirits first gets a sickness, a bad sickness. No one can become a sangoma who does not get this. You must tell people what happens to us, all the sangomas when that spirit calls them. Oh! How hard it is and how we must work with those spirits![19]

There are many parallels to shamanic themes in the life of Jesus. Although there is no evidence in the gospels that he experienced an initiatory illness, Jesus' forty-day ordeal in the wilderness prior to beginning his public life as an itinerant healer and teacher can be likened to a kind of shamanic initiation during which he personally "worked with the spirits."[20] From the perspective of shamanism, Jesus' assertive dealings with the temptations of the Satanic spirit in the wilderness would likely be seen as the source of his later power and "authority" over unclean spirits—which are often noted in the gospel accounts of his healings of tormented people. Jesus' visionary experiences in the wilderness (e.g., journeying with Satan to the top of a high mountain or to the pinnacle of the temple) are also reminiscent of the "soul journeys" or "spirit flights" of the shaman.

The gospels also suggest that, from the beginning of his public life, Jesus strongly identified with the mysterious "Suffering Servant of Yahweh" figure (the one who brings good news to the poor, heals the brokenhearted, brings liberty to captives) from the writings of the prophet Isaiah.[21] In Christianity, there is a long tradition of belief that Jesus was the fulfillment of this countercultural redemptive figure foretold by the prophet: the "man of sorrows" whose wounds would become a source of healing and redemption for others:

> Who has believed what we have heard? And to whom has the arm of the LORD been revealed? . . . He had no form or majesty that we should look at him, nothing in his appearance that we should desire him. He was despised and rejected by others; a man of suffering and acquainted with infirmity; and as one from whom others hide their faces he was despised, and we held him of no account.
>
> Surely he has borne our infirmities and carried our diseases; yet we accounted him stricken, struck down

by God, and afflicted. But he was wounded for our transgressions, crushed for our iniquities; upon him was the punishment that made us whole, and by his bruises we are healed.[22]

The image of the wounded healer also resonates deeply with many people who experience callings to compassionate service today. Many in the helping and healing professions are wounded healers who trace the early inklings of their own callings either to painful personal experiences or to close proximity to the pain of significant others at some point in their lives that sensitized them to suffering and awakened an interest in relieving it. Personal encounters with particular problems can give us an intimate, first-hand knowledge of what it is like to deal with them, what it takes to heal them. We become "familiar" with certain kinds of "infirmities" and develop a particular kind of wisdom and compassion about them.

Many people who work in the field of addiction recovery, for example, have themselves had a personal history of struggles with alcohol or drug addiction. They are familiar with the territory and know what it is like to have a drinking or drug problem. They have faced the "demon" and fought their way back to sobriety, and it is exactly this personal knowledge and experience that becomes one of their primary qualifications (not the only one) for helping others. Many in the mental health professions also can identify early stirrings of interest in the work of emotional healing with life experiences that forced them to become familiar with the territory of emotional suffering. Sanford has summarized the pattern:

Like the shamans, persons who are meant to work in the healing field are Wounded Healers. If a person has gone through a crisis, died to an old personality, and fought his or her way back to health, that person may gain a certain quality that enables him [or her] to put others in touch with healing too. A certain faith in the healing process is generated by having found healing oneself, not to mention a capacity for empathy with those who are ill, which can only come through having suffered.[23]

There are also wounded healers whose vocation extends beyond personal work with individuals to the work of healing in the wider social and political realm. Sister Dianna Ortiz is a striking example. An Ursuline nun from New Mexico, Ortiz journeyed to Guatemala in the early 1980s as a missionary to work as a teacher with Mayan children in the highlands. In November 1989, she was abducted, raped, and brutally tortured in a notorious military interrogation center in the capital city. The harrowing story of her torture and subsequent battles to recover her emotional health and personal dignity are recounted in the compelling memoir *The Blindfold's Eyes: My Journey from Torture to Truth*.[24]

A crucial component of Ortiz's healing process—which she likens to a traumatic experience of death and a slow and painful process of rebirth—has been her determination to *use* her personal experience of traumatic victimization for the benefit of others. She now works to help others (especially women) heal from the wounds of torture through building supportive "communities of healing" for torture survivors. She is also a human rights activist who works for the abolition of the practice of torture in the contemporary world. As a survivor of torture, Ortiz speaks with great personal conviction and authority as a wounded healer:

What I endured is the suffering of millions of women around the world. That I live now is testament to my rebirth—death by torture followed by rebirth. Torture's ghost walks beside me every step of the way, reminding me that the past will always be there.... I feel the need to give special attention to women who have suffered a fate similar to mine.... Our faith calls each of us to live out the gospel, and that gospel insists that, like Jesus, we speak truth to power. To speak the truth about the horrors of torture and to challenge government, church, and other leaders to denounce torture is simply my moral obligation, and, quite frankly, I believe it is the moral obligation of every human being on this planet.[25]

Cindy Sheehan, the grieving mother of an American soldier killed in Iraq, is another current example of a wounded healer whose calling has taken on a prophetic public dimension. After her son Casey was killed in action in April 2004, Sheehan helped to found the group "Gold Star Families for Peace" for families who had lost a loved one in the war. She began traveling around the country, sharing the story of her personal loss as a way of raising public consciousness about the terrible personal costs of the war. As I write, she is becoming the focus of considerable media attention as a result of her public protest against the war from her encampment on the outskirts of the presidential ranch in Crawford, Texas.[26]

There is a way in which Cindy Sheehan's dramatic public grieving at the doorstep of the president is a modern manifestation of the spirit of the prophets of old. In ancient Israel the prophet's task was to gain the ear of the king; Sheehan boldly insists on a personal meeting with the president so that he can be confronted with the reality of her grief and anguish. As if he were writing with the Texas protest in mind, Walter Brueggemann says that the language of lament and grief is the "proper idiom for the prophet in cutting through royal numbness and denial":

The task of the prophet is to invite the king to experience what he must experience, what he most needs
to experience and most fears to experience, namely,
that the end of the royal fantasy is very near.... I believe that the proper idiom for the prophet in cutting
through the royal numbness and denial is *the language
of grief,* rhetoric that engages the community in mourning for a funeral they do not want to admit. It is indeed their own funeral. I have been increasingly
impressed with the capacity of the prophet to use the
language of lament and the symbolic creation of a
death scene as a way of bringing to reality what the
king must see and will not. And I believe that grief
and mourning, that crying in pathos, is the ultimate
form of criticism, for it announces the sure end of the
whole royal arrangement.[27]

Whether by way of prophetic public efforts to heal a sick
society or through compassionate personal attention to the
hurt of individual persons, the wounded healer finds a way to
use his or her own pain for the benefit of others.

REDEMPTIVE SUFFERING

Suffering does not always have a redemptive outcome. Painful
life experiences have the potential to deepen and mature us,
to make us wiser and more compassionate, but this is not always how things work out. Pain can also make us numb or
bitter or self-absorbed. It can make us so preoccupied with
our own discomfort that we have little energy or interest left
over for anyone or anything beyond ourselves. Suffering can
soften the heart—or it can turn it to stone. And so we should
be careful not to romanticize or spiritualize suffering too

much, to assume that it will inevitably have ennobling or transformative effects upon our consciousness or character.

One factor that determines whether suffering will have a redemptive outcome is our *attitude* toward it. "Suffering by itself is no cure," says Sanford, "it only cures us when we have the right attitude toward it."[28] From this vantage point, the issue is not the particular form the trouble takes (e.g., illness, injury, depression, poverty, persecution) or even the degree of pain associated with it. Rather, what makes the difference is how we *look* at the difficulties life sends our way. How we see our problems has a profound impact upon how they are experienced, including the degree to which they are felt to be either meaningful opportunities for growth or meaningless obstacles that are better avoided.

The "right" attitude enables us to discern *meaning* in our sufferings. Meaning is what makes it possible for us to make spiritual sense of what otherwise seems senseless, to bear what would otherwise be unbearable. According to Victor Frankl, whether suffering becomes an occasion for spiritual triumph or defeat depends entirely on our capacity to discover a meaning or purpose in it. Frankl, an Austrian psychiatrist who wrote of his personal experiences of extreme suffering in the Nazi concentration camps in the classic *Man's Search for Meaning*, emphasized the human capacity to *choose* our attitude toward suffering regardless of external circumstances. "Everything can be taken away but one thing," he wrote, "the last of human freedoms—to choose one's attitude in any given set of circumstances.... Fundamentally, even in the worst of circumstances, we can decide what shall become of ourselves mentally and spiritually, retaining our human dignity even in a concentration camp."[29]

Finding the correct spiritual attitude in any given difficult situation determines whether we will experience it as a blessing or a curse. When we are contending with painful life problems, finding the blessing has to do with discovering the hidden spiritual meaning or message contained in the problem, the "blessing in disguise." The temptation is always to give up the struggle prematurely before we have learned what we need to learn, before we have "gotten" the message. The mysterious biblical story of Jacob's wrestling match with God gives us a glimpse of the kind of attitude required of those who would obtain the blessing:

> Jacob was left alone; and a man wrestled with him until daybreak. When the man saw that he did not prevail against Jacob, he struck him on the hip socket; and Jacob's hip was put out of joint as he wrestled with him. Then he said, "Let me go, for the day is breaking." But Jacob said, "I will not let you go, unless you bless me." So he said to him, "What is your name?" And he said, "Jacob." Then the man said, "You shall no longer be called Jacob, but Israel, for you have striven with God and with humans, and have prevailed." Then Jacob asked him, "Please tell me your name." But he said, "Why is it that you ask my name?" And there he blessed him. So Jacob called the place Peniel, saying, "For I have seen God face to face, and yet my life is preserved."[30]

The "I will not let you go, unless you bless me" attitude of Jacob is what keeps him fighting and struggling with his adversary long enough to receive the blessing, which, in his case, has to do with *learning who he is.* Jacob is given a new name, *Israel,* which means "Wrestler with God." He also ultimately learns the identity of the dark, mysterious adversary who has ambushed him: God. In my psychotherapeutic work, I have found many people to be mysteriously consoled and encouraged by this story when they are faced with discouraging and demoralizing life problems. They get the idea that it is worth "hanging in there" a little longer until the meaning of the issue or problem, the message in the symptom, can be discerned. This almost always involves allowing the suffering or pain to reveal and clarify the truth of *who they are*—a process that seems to be inherently healing and redemptive. Interestingly, Jacob is also wounded in the struggle with God; he limps for the rest of his days.

Another issue related to the redemptive potential of suffering is the extent to which any particular painful experience becomes an occasion for deepened loving connection with God or other human beings. In *The Saints' Guide to Happiness*, Robert Ellsberg reminds us of this *relational* dimension of the experience of suffering: "Even in the midst of grave misfortune there is access to God."[31] For many of us, one thing suffering seems to do quite effectively is to remind us of our *need* for God, for "access" or connection to a higher power that can save or deliver us from misfortune or danger.

In *The Varieties of Religious Experience,* William James offered his view of the universal underlying structure of the process of salvation or redemption—what he referred to as "the uniform deliverance in which religions all appear to meet":

The warring gods and formulas of the various religions do indeed cancel each other, but there is a certain uniform deliverance in which religions all appear to meet. It consists of two parts:

1. An *uneasiness*; and

2. Its *solution.*

> 1. The uneasiness, reduced to its simplest terms, is a sense that there is *something wrong about us* as we naturally stand.

> 2. The solution is a sense that we are *saved* from the wrongness by making proper connection with the higher powers.[32]

Victor Frankl's story offers a compelling example of the kind of "deliverance" James is talking about. For Frankl, the "uneasiness" or "wrongness" was the senseless cruelty and inhumanity of the concentration camp experience, which not only threatened the prisoners' physical survival but violated their basic human need and right to be treated as human beings worthy of respect and dignity. For Frankl, the "solution" to the uneasiness, the thing that *saved* him from the wrongness, was making "proper connection" with the higher power of love.

Concretely, Frankl's solution to the bleak and horrifying external reality of Auschwitz was to turn inwards, to recall and re-live loving memories of his wife prior to the Holocaust, and to have tender dialogues with her in his imagination: "My mind clung to my wife's image, imagining it with an uncanny acuteness. I heard her answering me, saw her smile, her frank and encouraging look."[33] These imagined conversations with his wife helped Frankl reconnect with the consoling, morale-building reality of love, to recover a sense of himself as a person *capable* of love and *worthy* of being loved:

> In a position of utter desolation, when a man cannot express himself in positive action, when his only achievement may consist in enduring his sufferings in the right way—an honorable way—in such a position a man can, through loving contemplation of the image he carries of his beloved, achieve fulfillment.[34]

Although Frankl did not know it at the time, his beloved wife had already been murdered in the gas chambers in another area of the camp months before. Ultimately, it didn't matter, because "love is as strong as death":

> I didn't even know if she was still alive. I only knew one thing—which I have learned well by now: Love goes very far beyond the physical person of the beloved. . . . Had I known then that my wife was dead, I think I would have still given myself, undisturbed by that knowledge, to the contemplation of her image, and that mental conversation with her would have been just as vivid and just as satisfying. "Set me as a seal upon thy heart, love is as strong as death."[35]

Frankl's tender inner conversations with his wife bear a striking resemblance to prayer—except, of course, that they involve a human partner instead of God. His "loving contemplation of the image of his beloved" allowed him to have access to her in spite of external circumstances, just as prayer can serve as a lifeline to God even in the midst of overwhelming pain and trouble. Human or divine, in the flesh or in the imagination, the sense of connection with the Other offers a blessed relief—not from suffering itself—but from bearing the burden of it in isolation. Access to the beloved makes possible a redemptive experience of shared suffering, a compassionate experience of "suffering with" in place of the crushing experience of suffering alone.

In the twenty centuries of the Christian tradition, contemplation of the image and reality of the crucified Jesus has served as a saving lifeline to God for suffering people. One evening, on a recent visit to Guatemala, I observed a group of very poor people in a church patiently waiting in line for their turn to pray in front of a life-sized statue of the crucified Jesus. Each person, in their turn, went to the foot of the cross, and, as they prayed quietly about whatever was on their minds or in their hearts, they reached up and literally *clung* to the legs of Jesus. From the looks of life-long suffering etched into their faces, I suspect that some were hanging on to him for dear life.

Although distorted forms of Christian piety can become morbidly preoccupied with the passion and death of Jesus, authentic Christian spirituality is not about suffering for its own sake. It is about the redemptive breakthrough of love and compassion *through* suffering, or in the midst of it, or in spite of it. "Amazing Grace! How sweet the sound that saved a wretch like me!" The crucified Jesus offers people an image of God that captures the heart and the imagination. This is a God with whom it is possible to connect—a *human* God, a God who suffers, a compassionate God who is able to appreciate what it is like to be a suffering human being. "For we do not have a high priest who is unable to sympathize with our weaknesses," reads the Letter to the Hebrews, "but . . . one who in every respect has been tested as we are, yet without sin."[36] The One who is able to sympathize or empathize with human weakness and pain is accessible, approachable: "Let us therefore approach the throne of grace with boldness, so that we may receive mercy and find grace to help in time of need."[37]

In a mysterious way, the crucified Jesus not only provides us with a concrete image of God's love and compassion for suffering humanity but also evokes compassion in *us* for the God who suffers. The image of the crucified Jesus gives us a feeling for the radical vulnerability and helplessness of God. We are touched and moved by the suffering of God. There is a give-and-take of compassion, an experience of shared suffering: God feels for *us* and we feel for *God*. The evocative words of the African American spiritual "Were You There?" capture this poignant feeling for many people:

Were you there when they crucified my Lord?
Oh, sometimes it causes me to tremble, tremble,
   tremble.
Were you there when they crucified my Lord?

The image of Jesus can also serve as a point of compassionate connection with suffering humanity, with the God who is suffering right now in suffering persons and in the "crucified peoples" of the world. We move from personal, private, inner contemplation of the suffering God into the world of social suffering, to the encounter with God in the lives of suffering human beings. We experience God very concretely in those whose pains and needs are crying out for our attention, in the experience of solidarity and sharing in their suffering, in our attempts to be of service in some way. "I am endeavoring to see God through service of humanity," wrote Gandhi, "for I know that God is neither in heaven, nor down below, but in everyone."[38]

"Blessed are the merciful," said Jesus, "for they will receive mercy."[39] It is in the exercise of mercy and compassionate action that we mysteriously experience ourselves as the recipients of God's tender mercy and compassion. Sobrino makes a link between mercy and justice, using the striking image of the "crucified peoples":

> We are speaking here not of the "works of mercy" but rather of the basic structure of the response to the world's victims. This structure consists of making someone else's pain our very own and allowing that pain to move us to respond. . . . We well know that in our world there are not just wounded individuals but crucified peoples, and that we should enflesh mercy accordingly. To react with mercy, then, means to do everything we possibly can to bring them down from

the cross. This means working for justice—which is
the name love acquires when it comes to entire ma-
jorities of people unjustly oppressed.[40]

"Making someone else's pain our own" through empathy
and compassion enables us to feel and imagine ourselves in
their world, to see and feel things from their vantage point. It
can even make it possible for us to cross over from our limited human viewpoint to the ultimate perspective of God, to
see this world and its troubles through God's eyes. For Christians, this is accomplished by way of the heart connection
with the merciful, forgiving Jesus. Perhaps the ultimate expression of Jesus' great mercy is his forgiving attitude toward
those who crucified him:

> When they came to the place that is called the Skull,
> they crucified Jesus there with the criminals, one on
> his right and one on his left. Then Jesus said, "Father,
> forgive them, for they do not know what they are
> doing."[41]

Even in the midst of his own torture, Jesus is able to give
his crucifiers the benefit of the doubt, to generously allow for
the possibility that they don't "get" it. "On behalf of the
world that has now sentenced him," says Brueggemann, Jesus
"enters *a plea of temporary insanity.*"[42] By crossing over to Jesus'
perspective, we are able to experience within ourselves something of the compassion and mercy of God for this insane
and sinful world in which we live. In the words of Flannery
O'Connor, we are able "to feel life from the standpoint of the
central Christian mystery: that it has, for all its horrors, been
found by God to be worth dying for."[43]

8

CONSCIENCE
The Morality of the Heart

In that most secret core of our being we are haunted by a moral siren summoning us to become more and more fully human, to transform ourselves into increasingly loving and principled adults, indeed, to become saints.
      —Russell B. Connors and Patrick T. McCormick[1]

TWO CHILDREN'S STORIES come to mind in connection with conscience. The first is from the classic movie version of *The Adventures of Pinocchio,* in which little Jiminy Cricket (a caricature of conscience in the popular imagination) sings his famous advice: "Always let your conscience be your guide." The second is a poignant scene from a more recent film, *The Land before Time.* Little Foot, the main character, is a heartbroken young dinosaur in terrible grief over the death of his mother. Wondering how he will ever get along without her, he is paid a consoling visit by the spirit of his deceased mother, who gives him some advice about how to find his way in the world: "Let your heart guide you," she says. "It whispers, so listen carefully."

In this chapter I want to bring together the notions of "conscience" and "heart," to develop an integrative perspective on the moral and affective dimensions of our experience, a "morality of the heart."[2] The unifying idea comes from theologian Enda McDonagh, who speaks of the "tug of the moral" in our lives.[3] One of the primary ways in which our conscience guides us, it seems, is through the "moral tug" upon our hearts. We hear it, *feel* it drawing or pulling us this way or that as we consider what we should do or how we should be in the world. The gospel song "Feel Something Drawing Me On" captures this beautifully:

> I feel something drawing, I feel it pulling, I feel it urging,
> I feel something drawing me on.
> There's something so divine, down in this heart of
>   mine,
> I feel something drawing me on.[4]

To ground these reflections on conscience in the feeling dimension of experience, I will begin with some thoughts on the notion of heart in the Bible. This will be followed by an exploration of some dimensions of the psychology and spirituality of conscience, including the complex phenomenon of guilt and the relationship of conscience and empathy. Finally, for the sake of illustration, I will look at a famous case example from *The Adventures of Huckleberry Finn* by Mark Twain.

THE INNER VOICE OF CONSCIENCE

Although there is no specific word for conscience in the Hebrew scriptures, the notion of something closely resembling conscience is clearly embodied in the biblical notion of the heart.[5] "You desire truth in the inward being," writes the Psalmist, "therefore teach me wisdom in my secret heart."[6] Theologically, it can be said that God *uses* the inclinations of our true self, the promptings of conscience, the wisdom of our "secret heart" to help and guide and call us through decisions big and small toward the goal or purpose for which we were created, the ever deeper and fuller sense of humanity that Connors and McCormick liken to *sainthood*.

God's word is heard *in* the heart, *by* the heart; God speaks *to* the heart, *through* the heart: "O that today you would listen to his voice! Do not harden your hearts, as at Meribah."[7] When Job is agonizing over whether he may have been responsible for bringing his misfortune and troubles upon himself, he searches his heart and finds that it does not "reproach" him in the way that would be expected in a person with a guilty conscience.[8] The prophet Jeremiah speaks of God's law being written *on* or *in* our hearts: "I will put my law within them, and I will write it on their hearts."[9] Connors and McCormick admire the wisdom of this heart-grounded biblical notion of morality:

> The genius of the biblical notion of the heart . . . is that it reminds us both that our conscience is the inner sanctum where we hear God's call to be good and do what is right, and that this call summons us to be our best selves, to be fully human persons and communities. As a result, conscience is the "place" within us where we face ourselves most profoundly and honestly, and the "place" where we discern how God calls us to do the truth. Conscience is us as we struggle to discern and respond to the "moral tug."[10]

In the Roman Catholic tradition, the notion of conscience is rooted in these central biblical images of a law or voice that can be detected or discerned in the deepest core of the human person. According to the bishops at Vatican II,

> In the depths of our conscience, we detect a law which we do not impose upon ourselves, but which

holds us to obedience. Always summoning us to love good and avoid evil, the voice of conscience when necessary speaks to our hearts: do this, shun that. For we have in our hearts a law written by God; to obey it is the very dignity of the human person; according to it we will be judged. Conscience is the most secret core and sanctuary of a person. There we are alone with God, whose voice echoes in our depths. In a wonderful manner conscience reveals that law which is fulfilled by love of God and neighbor. In fidelity to conscience, Christians are joined with the rest of people in the search for truth, and for the genuine solution to the numerous problems which arise in the life of individuals and from social relationships.[11]

Unfortunately, words like *obedience* or *law* used in conjunction with conscience have negative emotional and spiritual associations for many people. Instead of evoking rich images of the "secret core or sanctuary" of our being, the place where God's voice "echoes in our depths," what comes to mind is something more like the *superego*. This was Freud's term for the critical, rule-oriented voice in our heads, often associated with parental or religious or societal "shoulds," that tends to induce needless guilt and unproductive anxiety in us about things that do not matter. Moral theologian Richard Gula calls this confusion of the superego with the genuine inner voice of conscience the "conscience/superego mix-up."[12]

In Freud's original theory, the superego is a structure within the mind that develops through a normal psychological process of internalizing the moral norms we absorb from family, religion, and culture. These internalized standards of right and wrong eventually become our superego, which functions, for all intents and purposes, like the inner voice of conscience within our own minds. The content and emotional tone of our superego, i.e., *what* it says and *how* it says things, are determined by the unique character of our individual upbringing. For example, a person with relaxed, flexible parents would, according to Freud's theory, be expected to develop a correspondingly flexible superego, and consequently be less prone to anxiety and guilt and self-criticism.

On the other hand, a person with harsh, rigid, or punitive parents would be expected to develop a superego characterized by a correspondingly negative and critical tone. She might be more prone to hearing a critical or judgmental voice within herself, and consequently be more vulnerable to intense feelings of guilt and anxiety whenever she happens to think or feel or do the "wrong" thing. Freud himself expressed a kind of puzzlement and dismay over the potential for a rigid, critical superego to induce a neurotic sense of guilt in his patients: "How is it that the super-ego manifests itself as a sense of guilt (or rather, as criticism—for the sense of guilt is the perception in the ego answering to this criticism) and moreover develops such harshness and severity towards the ego?"[13]

Both in psychotherapy with guilt-ridden people and in vocational discernment, it is helpful to sort out the "conscience/superego mix-up" by making a distinction between the critical, rule-oriented superego and the true conscience. James Hillman, a disciple of Jung, provides a helpful perspective:

> [Jung] describes two forms of conscience. There is the conscience which we gain through learning, through the inculcation of values from our parents and our peers, from the traditional dogma of religion about right and wrong, and which we might call the superego. However, there is another sort of conscience,

because as he says, "The phenomenon of conscience in itself does not coincide with the moral code, but is anterior to it, transcends its contents...." The superego, the first sort of conscience, is, in fact, secondary. I mean by this that we can only take in certain principles and follow a moral code and obey our parents' and our religions' teachings because of the psychological faculty of conscience, the inborn capacity to feel guilt.... Conscience is the voice of self-guidance. The self-regulating, self-steering activity of the psyche gives conscience its authority.... Conscience, as an aspect of self-regulation, is the voice of the Self, which may and does conflict with the contents of a superego conscience.[14]

Using less technical language, John Sanford makes a distinction between the superego, which he calls the "Inner Critic," and the true conscience, which he calls the "voice of our real Self." In his view, the Inner Critic is a judgmental, accusatory inner voice that induces unhealthy feelings of anxiety and guilt, feelings that undermine our well-being and hold us back from making emotional and spiritual progress. Our true conscience, on the other hand, is experienced as a helpful, growth-promoting source of inner wisdom and guidance. When it corrects us, the criticism it offers from within is constructive and seems to have our best interests at heart.

Both the superego and the true conscience are capable of making us feel guilty. It seems, however, that these different voices generate different *kinds* of guilt that can either help or hinder our development as persons. It is to these different kinds of guilt that we now turn.

REAL AND FALSE GUILT

In his book *Voice Therapy*, Robert Firestone discusses the profoundly destructive and undermining impact that pathological forms of the negative superego voice can have. In severe cases, this can give rise to annihilating feelings of neurotic guilt, depression, worthlessness, despair, self-hatred, and inhibition of a person's natural inclinations toward emotional growth and self-realization.[15] The traditional religious term for such a rigid, overactive superego is "scruples," a problem that is manifested in obsessional, guilt-driven ways of thinking and behaving that give the superficial appearance of virtuousness, but which are actually pathological and self- destructive.

Firestone makes a useful distinction between "neurotic guilt" and "existential guilt." Both forms of guilt are generated by guilt-inducing inner voices, but they have different meanings and origins. Neurotic guilt, consistent with Freud's original theory, arises from the violation of superego standards or rules. Existential guilt, by contrast, arises not when we have betrayed our superego, but when we have betrayed *ourselves.* In this sense, we are guilty of being *inauthentic,* of going against our own inner nature. Irving Yalom, a psychologist in the tradition of existential psychology, says it this way: "Most simply put: One is guilty not through transgressions against another or some moral or social code, but *one may be guilty of transgressing against oneself.*"[16] In contrast to destructive forms of the rule-oriented superego voice that induce neurotic guilt and inhibition, the source of existential guilt is a *constructive* inner voice that "corrects" us from within when we have deviated or strayed from our authentic path in life—when we have not been true to ourselves. According to Yalom, "existential guilt is a positive force...a guide *calling oneself back to oneself.*"[17]

In the Jungian tradition, Sanford makes a similar distinction between what he calls "false guilt" and "real guilt."[18] In his view, false guilt is comparable to neurotic guilt. False guilt is induced by the superego-like voice he calls the Inner Critic. Real guilt, on the other hand, corresponds closely with existential guilt, and is seen as stemming from our true conscience or the "voice of our real Self." Our true conscience offers us constructive criticism and guidance from within; it is like the voice that "calls oneself back to oneself":

> There is indeed a true Conscience within us, a voice that can be said to come from our real Self and that tries to correct us when we deviate from our proper path in life. When this voice comes to us we need to listen. But corrections from this voice do not annihilate us. Painful though such corrections may be, they lead us back to our true Self, not away from it. For these corrections come, not from false guilt feelings, but from a violation of our true and deepest nature. When we deviate from our true nature, we hear what amounts to the voice of God within us.[19]

In the Christian tradition, the painful corrective experience of real or existential guilt has been referred to as the "sting of conscience." The challenge in discernment has to do with the complex task of differentiating real guilt originating in the true conscience from false guilt originating in the superego. Such subtle distinctions between different kinds of guilt and their sources are not unlike the distinctions in Ignatian spirituality between feeling states associated with the different influences of good and evil spirits. For example, in his "Rules for the Discernment of Spirits," Ignatius Loyola suggests that the evil spirit tends to stir up discouraging feelings of false doubt and anxiety (false or neurotic guilt) in people who are on the path of genuine spiritual progress and growth.[20] In people who are moving in the wrong direction, by contrast, the good spirit is seen as arousing feelings of genuine remorse (real or existential guilt) which are experienced as the sting of conscience.[21]

My clinical work often involves helping guilt-ridden people to sort out and clarify the difference between real and false guilt, which are often quite intertwined and confused and operate in unhelpful ways on an unconscious level. Many good people are heavily burdened and held back from authentic living by the emotional baggage of false guilt. For them, moving in the direction of emotional and spiritual health can feel like *sinning* because they tend to hear a critical, guilt-inducing inner voice whenever they think of taking a step toward authenticity. Their task is to liberate themselves from the grip of false guilt so that they can begin to follow the call of their true conscience. On the other hand, contrary to the popular caricature of psychology as promoting a guilt-free existence, there are times when we *should* feel guilty, when self-confrontation with our own sinfulness or inauthenticity is a painful but necessary step toward emotional, spiritual, and moral health.

Although the first thing that tends to come to many people's minds when they hear the word *obedience* is a kind of guilty submission to external authority, there are other ways to look at obedience that are less burdened with unhelpful emotional baggage. Interestingly, the Latin root of the word obedience is *audire,* which means "to listen."[22] In matters of conscience and calling, everything depends on our capacities to listen, discern, and follow the Voice. First of all, we must be able to *hear* it, which requires deep and careful listening for the often mysterious and unexpected ways in which it speaks from within ourselves and through our life experiences. Ultimately, after all our listening and discerning, we face the chal-

lenge of making intelligent and courageous choices to *follow*
where the Voice is leading us.

Taking the risk of saying "Yes" to a call is itself a form of
obedience, in the sense not of submitting to a law or expectation imposed upon us by external authority but of surren-
dering ourselves to the *internal* authority of our true self, our
conscience, our "secret heart." We obey by letting the Voice
guide our choices, by allowing it to have a say in our lives.
Following a call, in this sense, is a way of being *true* to ourselves. Jung calls this "fidelity to the law of one's own being."[23]
Dag Hammarskjold, secretary general of the United Nations
from 1953 until his death in a plane crash in 1961, describes
this kind of "yes" in a famous entry writen in his diary a few
months before he died:

> I don't know Who—or What—put the question, I
> don't know when it was put. I don't even remember
> answering. But at some moment I did answer *Yes* to
> Someone—or Something—and from that hour I was
> certain that existence is meaningful and that, there-
> fore, my life, in self-surrender, had a goal.[24]

THE SOUND HEART
AND THE DEFORMED CONSCIENCE

Conscience is not only about guilt. It is also about love and
compassion, because the right thing to do is usually the *loving*
thing to do. The "moral tug" pulls us toward becoming ever
more loving and compassionate persons. The moral person,
therefore, is the person who "has a heart."[25]

There is a connection between empathy and conscience.
"Having a heart" has to do with our capacity for empathy,
our ability to feel or imagine ourselves into the world of oth-

ers so that we can appreciate what things look and feel like from their perspective. According to Richard Gula, the capacity for empathy is the foundation for moral sensitivity and concern for the rights and feelings of others:

> Without the capacity for an affective experience of the value of persons and what befits their well-being, we will not have the capacity for acting in good conscience. The capacity for loving is the beginning of moral awareness. Research on the role of empathy shows how important this human feeling is in the development of conscience. Empathy is experiencing what another is experiencing. When empathy is born, care is born, and with it, morality.[26]

And so the formation of conscience is also a kind of education or schooling of the heart. Ideally, the morality we internalize will be in alignment with our true conscience or "natural heart." Problems arise, however, when there is a "conscience/superego mix-up," when there is too great a discrepancy between our superego and our true conscience. Rigid or unhealthy forms of superego morality (and the false guilt that accompanies them) can limit or impair our capacity for empathy and appropriate human feeling for others. The noisy static created by our Inner Critic can make it harder to hear the whisperings of our true conscience, which often speaks through the stirrings of empathy in our hearts. A *deformation* of conscience results when we internalize a narrow, rigid, unfeeling form of morality that conflicts with the compassionate inclinations of our natural hearts.

Mark Twain's classic *The Adventures of Huckleberry Finn* is the story of a boy with a good heart and sound moral instincts whose upbringing in a racist culture has *deformed* his conscience. The book chronicles Huck's adventures with Jim, a runaway slave who becomes Huck's friend as they make their way together up the Mississippi River to freedom in the North after Jim has escaped from slavery in the pre–Civil War American South. Huck's narration of his profound moral ambivalence and inner conflict over whether he should be breaking the law and helping Jim to freedom is at the heart of the story. The book itself is controversial and is seen as offensive by some African Americans because of its accurate depiction of the hateful racist thinking and language of the period.

Some years after the publication of the book in 1884, Twain wrote in his journal that *"Huck Finn* is a book of mine where a sound heart and a deformed conscience come into collision and conscience suffers defeat."[27] By "conscience," Twain means the twisted morality that Huck was taught in his Christian Sunday school, which included the notion that anyone who helped slaves to freedom would be punished by God in the "everlasting fire" of hell. The conscience/superego mix-up is evident in the mislabeling of Huck's racist superego morality as his "conscience." By "sound heart," on the other hand, Twain means to capture all of Huck's natural tendencies to see Jim as a human being (rather than as something *less* than human, i.e., "property" that should be returned to its owner), which are based more in his heartfelt sense of loyalty and friendship with Jim and his spontaneous inclinations to help him. The sound heart, of course, is more akin to the true conscience or natural heart.

Huck is tormented by a terrible sense of guilt over his efforts to help Jim. He is acutely conscious that he is violating not only the law of the land but also the moral law of his own conscience.[28] "The more I studied about this," says Huck, "the more my conscience went to grinding me, and the more wicked and low-down and ornery I got to feeling."[29] Sadly, Huck seems to interpret his friendly and empathic feelings toward Jim as evidence of his own personal moral weakness and wickedness. He is terrified that the very salvation of his soul may be at stake in the matter, and becomes obsessed with the idea that God is going to send him to hell for helping Jim to escape from slavery. Finally, Huck tries to pray:

> I made up my mind to pray; and see if I couldn't try to quit being the kind of boy I was, and be better. So I kneeled down. But the words wouldn't come. Why wouldn't they? . . . It was because my heart warn't right; it was because I warn't square; it was because I was playing double. . . . So I was full of trouble, full as I could be; and I didn't know what to do.[30]

Unable to tolerate his anxiety and guilt any longer, Huck decides that he must turn Jim in to the local authorities and write a letter to the slaveowner, informing her of Jim's whereabouts. After finishing the letter, he feels an initial sense of relief: "I felt good and all washed clean of sin . . . [about] how near I come to being lost and going to hell."[31] Then, however, he begins to think of his friendship with Jim, recalling Jim's affection for him and goodness *to* him, the joys of their adventures together. He remembers Jim's gratitude to him for helping to conceal him from the authorities, and how, at this point, he is really the only friend Jim has in the world. This, for Huck, is the moment of truth. In the most famous passage of the book, Huck looks at the letter he has written to the slaveowner and thinks to himself:

> It was a close place. I took it [the letter] up, and held it in my hand. It was a-trembling, because I'd got to decide, forever, betwixt two things, and I knowed it. I studied a minute holding my breath, and then says to

myself: "All right, then, I'll *go* to hell"—and tore it up.[32]

In his article "The Conscience of Huckleberry Finn," philosopher Jonathan Bennett sees the collision between Huck's deformed conscience and his sound heart as the conflict between his bad morality (i.e., the racist morality he had internalized) and his sympathy (i.e., empathy). "Huck's morality," he says, "conflicts with his sympathy, that is, with his unargued, natural feeling for his friend.... In this conflict between sympathy and morality, sympathy wins."[33] Compassionate feeling for Jim leads Huck to reject the narrow and cruel morality of his upbringing.

"What Huck rejects," says author Azar Nafisi, "is not religion but an attitude of self-righteousness and inflexibility." Nafisi, an Iranian-born Muslim who was fired from the University of Tehran because of her religious differences with the fundamentalist administration of her university, considers the universal lessons on empathy and conscience found in the story of Huck Finn in an essay titled "The Mysterious Connections That Link Us Together":

> I believe in empathy.... Only curiosity about the fate of others, the ability to put ourselves in their shoes, and the will to enter their world through the magic of imagination, creates this shock of recognition. Without this empathy there can be no genuine dialogue, and we as individuals and nations will remain isolated and alien, segregated and fragmented.... I believe that it is only through empathy that the pain experienced by an Algerian woman, a North Korean dissident, a Rwandan child or an Iraqi prisoner, becomes real to me and not just passing news. And it is at times like this when I ask myself, am I prepared—like Huck Finn—to give up Sunday school heaven for the kind of hell that Huck chose?[34]

Our very souls *are* at stake in matters of conscience and compassion, but in a different way than Huck Finn imagined. The kind of hell that Huck chose was actually not a hell at all. Huck chose to honor the compassionate stirrings of his own heart, feelings that mysteriously linked him to a runaway slave who became a brother and a friend. Following the inclinations of our natural heart is the true path to salvation.

9

SOCIAL CONSCIENCE
Awakening from the Sleep of Inhumanity

The fundamental change . . . consists of an awakening, but from another type of sleep, or better, from a nightmare—the sleep of inhumanity. It is the awakening to the reality of an oppressed and subjugated world, a world whose liberation is the basic task of every human being, so that in this way human beings may finally come to be human.
—Jon Sobrino[1]

"IT'S NOT RIGHT!" is the natural response of a sound heart to injustice and inhumanity. The unsettling emotional responses evoked in us by social suffering usually consist of some combination of compassion and indignation.[2] Such feelings, I think, are the emotional reverberations of social conscience within us. The experiences that stir such feelings are *wake-up calls*. If we allow ourselves to be affected by such experiences, they have the potential to soften our stony hearts and arouse our sleepy consciences, to awaken us, as Sobrino says, from the "sleep of inhumanity." They remind us of the common humanity we share with the sufferers and of our social responsibility to do as much as we possibly can to relieve their suffering.

Personal and social conscience are distinct but overlapping dimensions of the same inner voice. In this chapter I will focus on some of the social dimensions of conscience in the contemporary world, particularly the problem of needless human suffering caused by unjust poverty and unjust wars. I will begin by looking at the idea that persons of conscience are called to make an "option for the poor." This will be followed by an exploration of some disturbing moral questions raised by the so-called "War on Terror" in the post-9/11 world, especially by the war in Iraq and the practice of torture. In a global situation of expanding injustice and inequality, and in a nation caught up in a war regarded as unwise and unjust by most of the world, an uneasy conscience may be one of the best places to listen for the whisper of the Spirit that calls us to a better way.

OPTION FOR THE POOR

The phrase "preferential option for the poor" originated in the Latin American Catholic Church in the last few decades of the twentieth century, but the spirit of this "option" is as old as the Hebrew prophets and the gospels. "The Spirit of the Lord is upon me," read Jesus from the words of the prophet Isaiah, "because he has anointed me to bring good news to the poor."[3] The good news is that God is not neutral about the plight of the poor. Rather, God *prefers* the poor and takes their side in their struggles against unjust poverty and oppression:

> He has brought down the powerful from their
>   thrones,
>   and lifted up the lowly.
> He has filled the hungry with good things,
>   and sent the rich away empty.[4]

In *Opting for the Poor: The Challenge for North Americans,* Peter Henriot traces the history of the phrase "preferential

option for the poor," which came into common use as a result of two important conferences of the Latin American
bishops in Medellín, Columbia (1968) and Puebla, Mexico
(1979). At Puebla, the bishops stated that they wanted to take
up "a clear and prophetic option expressing preference for,
and solidarity with, the poor. We affirm the need for conversion on the part of the whole church to a preferential option
for the poor, an option aimed at their integral liberation."[5]

The adjective "preferential" suggests a definite bias in
favor of the poor. It does not necessarily suggest a bias against
the rich or the privileged, although it should unsettle all rich
and privileged people and lead to a searching examination of
conscience on their part. Rather, says Brazilian theologian
Leonardo Boff, "the church's option is a preferential option
for the poor, *against their poverty.*"[6] Also, in the original phrase,
the word "option" is not meant to suggest that solidarity with
and commitment to the poor is "optional." Actually, it is seen
as *essential* and *integral* to the Christian life. Whether or not
one is a practicing Christian, it can also be considered essential
to *human* life in "a world whose liberation is the basic task of
every human being, so that in this way human beings may finally come to be human."[7] Gustavo Gutiérrez, who is considered the founder of liberation theology, explains what is
meant by "the poor":

> The term *poverty* refers to the real poor.... The pov-
> erty to which the option refers is material poverty.
> Material poverty means premature and unjust death.
> The poor person is someone who is treated as a non-
> person, someone who is considered insignificant from
> an economic, political, and cultural point of view. The
> poor count as statistics; they are the nameless. But
> even though the poor remain insignificant within so-
> ciety, they are never insignificant before God.[8]

The option for the poor is about allowing the insignificant, nameless statistics to become "significant others" to us. We are invited to cultivate a personal relationship with the non-persons, to share our fate or "throw in our lot" with the poor:

> *Con los pobres de la tierra, quiero yo mi suerte echar.*
>> (With the poor people of the earth I want to throw
>>> in my lot)
> *El arroyo de la sierra, me complace mas que el mar.*
>> (The little mountain stream pleases me more than
>>> the sea)[9]

All of us are called to opt for the poor, to open our hearts to the poor, to do something with our lives that will make a difference for the better in *theirs*. The secret to salvation, to realizing our full humanity, is to find our own way to exercise this option in a meaningful way. Concretely, there are many ways to do this. Some do it by devoting their professional careers to some form of direct service to the poor. They find ways to contribute their skills and knowledge to alleviating the suffering of the poor through working directly with poor people or with organizations that serve the poor.

Although not everyone is called to full-time service to the poor, all of us are called to be mindful of the poor and to respond to the call to translate our compassionate feelings and good intentions into concrete actions on their behalf. This could be through some form of regular personal contact with the poor, through contributing money or raising funds for projects that benefit the poor, through efforts to raise consciousness about issues of poverty and social justice in our families and schools and churches and communities, or through political advocacy to advance public policy initiatives that help the poor or that change social structures that keep people poor.

Another concrete way that privileged North Americans can opt for the poor is through simplifying our lives and by making more discerning choices about how we use our money. This is good for our spiritual health, of course, because it helps us to live more centered and less cluttered and materialistic lives. Even more important, it is good for our moral health because by living more simply we are less likely to unwittingly participate in mindless, wasteful cultural habits of overconsumption that exploit and hurt and deprive the poor. "Live simply," as the saying goes, "so that others may simply live."

The point is not just to waste less money on unnecessary food and "stuff" that we don't really need but rather to be ever-mindful that people all over the world are desperately in need of our help at every moment. And the implication is that we should use the money we save to help the poor, to *give it away* to people who need it more than we do. Arthur Simon, one of the founders of Bread for the World, presents a number of thoughtful and compelling arguments for what he calls "scaling back":

> There are several arguments to be made in favor of scaling back. The first is that it is simply better for us. It can mean reduced stress, less rushing, fewer distractions, more time for friends and family, and a chance to refocus life on things that matter. . . . A second case to be made for simpler living is that it is kinder to God's creation. . . . A third argument...is that living simply may enable people who are barely surviving to live. Simpler living does that, however, only if you transfer resources to people whose lives are at risk. Eating less and spending less on food, for example, might be good for your health. . . . But cutting back isn't going to feed anyone unless, say, you

contribute the amount saved to a food bank, a relief or development agency, or a group advocating for hungry people.[10]

Throwing in our lot with the poor will *cost* us in one way or another. If we take the option for the poor seriously, it will cost us financially because we will be continually challenged to think of creative ways to transfer resources to people who need them much more than we do. We are called to "put our money where our mouth is." This is only fair, because, according to the biblical vision of justice, we are actually just giving back to the poor what didn't really belong to us in the first place.

There is also an emotional cost to involvement with the poor. Neil Altman, a psychologist who devoted a good part of his professional career to caring for inner city children and families in the South Bronx neighborhood of New York City, has described how such contact with the poor can make professionals vulnerable to the unsettling experience of feelings that mirror the painful feelings of the people with whom they are working. "The upper-middle-class therapist who goes to work in an inner city public clinic," he says, "frequently enters, psychologically, a realm of trauma and loss that she may have been able to avoid, to some degree, in her own life."[11] Consequently, she may find herself experiencing "more than the usual doses of anger, fear, and despair." She thereby gets a vicarious experience of the feelings that are the daily emotional lot of the poor. From this perspective, the burnout of people who work with the poor is an understandable by-product of the exhaustion and demoralization of the poor themselves.

In some places, opting for the poor is a life-and-death matter that can cost people their *life*. Archbishop Oscar Romero of El Salvador, who himself paid the ultimate price of martyrdom for taking sides with the abused poor of his homeland, spoke these sobering words just a month before his assassination in March 1980:

> Believe me, brothers and sisters, anyone committed to the poor must suffer the same fate as the poor. And in El Salvador we know the fate of the poor: to be taken away, to be tortured, to be jailed, to be found dead.[12]

Maryknoll Sister Ita Ford, one of four U.S. women who were brutally murdered by the El Salvadoran military later the same year, said that some are called to "put their *bodies* where their mouths are."[13] She and her companions (Maura Clarke, Dorothy Kazel, and Jean Donovan) were found in a lonely grave by the side of a road. In El Salvador at that time, it was a life-threatening matter to be a friend of the poor. "No one has greater love than this, to lay down one's life for one's friends."[14]

Although most of us, God willing, will not literally be called upon to lay down our lives for the poor, all of us should expect that there will be a cost to our discipleship if we take the option for the poor seriously. But we are also promised a great treasure for our efforts:

> "Good Teacher," asked the rich young man, "What must I do to inherit eternal life?" . . . Jesus, looking at him, loved him and said, "You lack one thing: go, sell what you own, and give the money to the poor, and you will have treasure in heaven; then come, follow me."[15]

THE WAR ON TERROR
AND THE CALL OF CONSCIENCE

The 9/11 tragedy continues to have profound emotional, spiritual, and political repercussions in our individual lives and in the collective life of our nation and our world. As a United States citizen, I shared in the widespread sense of shock and trauma in the aftermath of that terrible September day. I have also shared in the widespread sense of uneasiness, shame, and horror at the direction my country has taken in the post-9/11 world, and find myself increasingly preoccupied with issues of conscience raised by our conduct of the so-called "War on Terror."

The 9/11 attacks initially called forth a poignant outpouring of good will and solidarity among Americans and from around the world. Not long afterwards, though, a darker, meaner spirit seemed to take possession of our country's political life. The trauma that had brought out the best in us quickly began to bring out the *worst*. It was as if the words of Yeats were coming true in the post-9/11 world:

> Things fall apart; the center cannot hold;
> Mere anarchy is loosed upon the world,
> The blood-dimmed tide is loosed, and everywhere
> The ceremony of innocence is drowned;
> The best lack all conviction, while the worst
> Are full of passionate intensity.[16]

The unholy fruits of this loosing of the "blood-dimmed tide" are evident in the relentless bloody mayhem set in motion by the U.S. invasion and occupation of Iraq and in the mounting scandals arising from the apparently widespread practice of torture at U.S. military prisons in places like Abu Ghraib in

Iraq, Bagram Air Force Base in Afghanistan, and Guantanamo Bay, Cuba. Sadly, in just a few short years, our country has developed a notorious reputation for arrogance, belligerence, hypocrisy, and contempt for human rights and international law. Since 9/11, we have witnessed what James Carroll has called the "slow-motion wreck of American values."[17]

According to Cornel West, the 9/11 tragedy presented a painful but potentially redemptive opportunity for an honest, searching examination of our national conscience:

> The ugly events of 9/11 should have been an opportunity for national self-scrutiny. In the wake of the shock and horror of those attacks, many asked the question, why do they hate us? But the country failed to engage in a serious, sustained, deeply probing examination of the possible answers to that question.[18]

Unfortunately, this humbling opportunity for national self-scrutiny was largely missed. Instead of becoming wiser and better, our country became a selfish and violent bully on the world playground. "In much of the world," laments Bob Herbert, "the image of the United States . . . has morphed from an idealized champion of liberty to a heavily armed thug in camouflage fatigues. America is increasingly being seen as a dangerously arrogant military power that is due for a comeuppance."[19]

Our national arrogance reflects more than just an image problem, however. Our lack of humility is symptomatic of a deeper spiritual problem. In 1967, as the Vietnam War was escalating, Martin Luther King Jr. spoke about our country's arrogance at that particular historical moment in hard words that could just as well be addressed to us today:

> Don't let anybody make you think that God chose America as His divine messianic force to be a sort of policeman of the whole world. God has a way of

standing before the nations with judgment, and it seems that I can hear God saying to America: "You are too arrogant! If you don't change your ways, I will rise up and break the backbone of your power, and I'll place it in the hands of a nation that doesn't even know my name."[20]

Psychiatrist Robert Jay Lifton has coined a new diagnostic term for what is ailing America: "superpower syndrome."[21] Although our country has been troubled by symptoms of this condition before, it seems to have taken a marked turn for the worse and developed a more malignant and life-threatening character, both for ourselves and others, in the years since 9/11.

The torture and maltreatment of detainees in U.S. military prisons around the world is a symptom of "superpower syndrome."[22] My work as a psychologist includes some involvement with a program that serves immigrants from around the world who are survivors of torture in their home countries. Many of these immigrants suffer terribly from symptoms of post-traumatic stress disorder. In a newspaper interview with several of these people not long after the hideous photos of tormented Iraqi prisoners from Abu Ghraib were on the cover of every newspaper, it was reported that they had experienced setbacks in their own recovery because of the nightmarish personal memories these photos had triggered in them. Their faith in America as a place that promised safe refuge from such horrors had also been shaken. "I always wanted America to be morally super," said one man with a traumatic personal history of torture, "not just a superpower."[23] His comments echo the disappointment and grief of many Americans today.

Joseph Darby was the young U.S. soldier who "blew the whistle" at the Abu Ghraib prison by speaking up to his commanding officer about the torture and cruel maltreatment of Iraqi prisoners he had witnessed. "I knew I had to do something," said Darby in his testimony. "I didn't want to see any more prisoners being abused because I knew it was wrong."[24] In spite of fears of retaliation from other soldiers, this single act of humanity and moral courage by a young soldier whose conscience was bothering him continues to have profound and potentially redemptive repercussions around the world.

The prognosis for a national recovery from superpower syndrome is guarded at the present time, mainly because of our difficulty in facing up to our collective moral responsibility for the unfolding disaster in Iraq:

> To the mounting horror of the world, the United States of America is relentlessly bringing about the systematic destruction of a small, unthreatening nation for no good reason. Why has this not gripped the conscience of this country? . . . Something deeply shameful has us in its grip. We carefully nurture a spirit of detachment toward the wars we pay for. But that means we cloak ourselves in cold indifference to the unnecessary suffering of others—even when we cause it. We don't look at any of this directly because the consequent guilt would violate our sense of ourselves as nice people.[25]

Some signs of hope and potential for healing can be seen in the large numbers of people around the world who seem to be experiencing what can only be called a *vocation* to engage in a variety of forms of principled opposition and dissent against the misguided and destructive policies of our national government. Initial inklings of such callings are likely to be experienced on an emotional level, e.g., through feelings of anxiety, anger, shame, guilt, or grief in response to the senselessness of the Iraq War. Such feelings are the emotional echoes of the inner voice of conscience resonating in the minds and hearts of many people today.

It may be that one of the most urgent callings currently being extended to us as global citizens is the challenge of discerning creative ways in which we can personally contribute to the effort to help our country to recover its moral bearings. "Perhaps a new spirit is rising among us," said Dr. King. "If it is, let us trace its movements well and pray that our own inner being may be sensitive to its guidance, for we are deeply in need of a new way beyond the darkness that seems so close all around us."[26]

THE CALL TO SPEAK

As a general rule, actions speak louder than words: "Let us love, not in word or speech, but in truth and action."[27] Authentic callings bear fruit in some form of action or service that makes a difference for the better in the lives of real people. In the Christian tradition, "good works" are seen as the outward, behavioral manifestation of an authentic and sincere inner faith:

> What good is it, my brothers and sisters, if you say you have faith but do not have works? . . . If a brother or sister is naked and lacks daily food, and one of you says to them, "Go in peace; keep warm and eat your fill," and yet you do not supply their bodily needs, what is the good of that? So faith by itself, if it has no works, is dead.[28]

Although empty words can be used as an excuse for non-action, there are times when speaking up or speaking out is a genuine expression of loving action or service on behalf of others. There are times when we are *called* to speak, when love or justice or truth requires that we say something, that we let it be known through our words or our actions exactly where we stand. For example, in the build-up to the American invasion of Iraq, five members of my church community were arrested for civil disobedience because of their participation in a prayerful, nonviolent sit-in at the local federal building in Chicago. The intention of their action was to say a clear "No" to business as usual, which, at that time, included preparation for an unjustified attack on another country that would result, as we have seen, in the tragic deaths of tens of thousands of innocent people.

Speak Truth to Power is the title of an inspiring recent collection of stories about courageous men and women who have risked their lives speaking up for human rights.[29] Oscar Romero spoke hard truths to the powerful of El Salvador, not because he liked confrontation, but out of his great love for the people who had no voice and no power. He became known as the "voice for the voiceless" of El Salvador. Live weekly radio broadcasts of his Sunday homilies, in which he would publicly review and denounce the human rights abuses of the previous week, were a profound, morale-boosting experience of solidarity for the victimized poor of his country. These broadcasts endeared him to the poor, but they shamed and angered the government and the military to the point that he was eventually assassinated to punish and silence him for using his voice to such wonderful effect.

Keeping silent when we have the opportunity to speak up on behalf of truth or peace or justice sometimes constitutes a betrayal of our own conscience. In the mid-1960s, as the tragic waste and carnage of the Vietnam War was mounting, Martin Luther King Jr. became increasingly troubled by his own silence on this huge moral issue. Finally, he was moved to "break the betrayal of his own silences" and to "speak from the burnings of his own heart" in a prophetic public denunciation of the war at Riverside Church in New York City in April 1967, where he spoke of the "calling to speak":

> Some of us who have already begun to break the silence of the night have found that the calling to speak is often a vocation of agony, but we must speak. We must speak with all the humility that is appropriate to our limited vision, but we must speak. And we must rejoice as well, for this is the first time in our nation's history that a significant number of its religious leaders have chosen to move beyond the prophesying of smooth patriotism to the high grounds of a firm dissent based on the mandates of conscience and the reading of history.[30]

Next to the soaring eloquence of a heroic person like Martin Luther King Jr., we may fear that our own halting voices and modest efforts on behalf of peace and justice are of little or no significance. This kind of thinking, however, gets us nowhere because it disparages and diminishes our own God-given voices and our own potential to make a real difference in the world. When we are feeling discouraged and inadequate, it is good to remember the story of "Nothing More Than Nothing":

> "Tell me the weight of a snowflake," a coal mouse asked a wild dove. "Nothing more than nothing," was the answer.
> "In that case I must tell you a marvelous story," the coal mouse said. "I sat on a branch of a fir, close to its trunk, when it began to snow—not heavily, not in a giant blizzard, no, just like in a dream, without any violence. Since I didn't have anything better to do, I counted the snow-flakes settling on the twigs

and needles of my branch. Their number was exactly 3,741,952. When the next snowflake dropped onto the branch—nothing more than nothing—as you say—the branch broke off." Having said that, the coal mouse scurried away.

The dove, since Noah's time an authority on the matter, thought about the story for a while and finally said to herself: "Perhaps there is only one person's voice lacking for peace to come into the world."[31]

10

CONCLUSION
A Still and Quiet Conscience

I know myself now, and I feel within me a peace above all earthly dignities, a still and quiet conscience.
　　—William Shakespeare
　　The Life of King Henry the Eighth[1]

The choice does not lie between the good conscience of a self which has kept all its laws and a bad conscience of the transgressor, but between the dull conscience which does not discern the greatness of the other and the holiness of [God's] demands, the agonized conscience of the awakened, and the consoled conscience of one who in the company of the Spirit seeks to fulfill the infinite demands of the infinite other.
　　—H. Reinhold Niebuhr[2]

THE HEART OF THE MATTER is finding a way to live on this earth "in good conscience." When we are living in good conscience, we are at peace with ourselves and with God. No matter what difficulties or challenges may be presenting themselves on the surface of our lives, at a deeper level of the soul we sense something of what Shakespeare called the "peace above all earthly dignities," what Ignatius Loyola called "consolation." We feel the kind of peace and joy that are referred to in the Christian tradition as the "fruits of the Spirit."[3]

In this concluding chapter I want to explore a few final themes. The first is the complex matter of how we measure "success" in matters of vocation and conscience. Another issue is the inherent sense of risk and uncertainty that goes with the territory of vocational discernment, especially the concern that we might make mistakes in important decisions about our lives. Finally, I will conclude with some thoughts on the weighty matters of love and death. In a nutshell, death is a sober reminder that the only thing that really matters, in the end, is love.

SUCCESS AND FAILURE

"The term 'vocation,'" writes Daniel Berrigan, "is not to be confused, as it commonly is, with a successful outcome."[4] But how do we measure success in matters of vocation and conscience?

To start with, although career and calling often overlap, it can help to make distinctions between them. According to William Sloane Coffin: "A career seeks to be successful, a calling to be valuable. A career tries to make money, a calling tries to make a difference."[5] Holy people all over the world are quietly going about the business of doing valuable things that make a difference all the time. Though most of them make very little money and never make the newspapers, they are, nonetheless, successful in the eyes of God.

By conventional cultural standards, success is measured by the yardstick of "upward mobility." The call of compassion, however, sometimes beckons us in a countercultural direction. Contrary to our expectation that we will be carried upwards, we experience instead an unsettling *downward* pull. In their book *Compassion*, Nouwen, McNeill, and Morrison reflect on this disconcerting theme of "downward mobility" in the life and message of Jesus:

Jesus' compassion is characterized by a downward pull.
That is what disturbs us. We cannot even think of
ourselves in terms other than those of the upward
pull, an upward mobility in which we strive for better lives, higher salaries, and more prestigious posi-
tions. Thus we are deeply disturbed by a God who
embodies a downward movement.[6]

The gospels suggest that Jesus was not a social climber by
any stretch, that he was remarkably unconcerned with status,
money, security, prestige, and power. A profoundly humble
person, he spent most of his time with people at the *bottom* of
the social ladder. The downward pull is in the direction of
the poor, the nobodies, the "least" and the "last." Ignatius
Loyola saw Jesus as the perfect embodiment of what he called
"loving humility" (*humildad amorosa*). In his reflections on
"Three Ways of Being Lovingly Humble," Ignatius suggested
that, for those who aspire to follow the example of Jesus, the
most "perfect" form of humility consists in this:

In order to imitate Christ our Lord better and to be
more like him in the here and now, I desire and
choose poverty with Christ poor rather than wealth;
contempt with Christ laden with it rather than hon-
ors. Even further, I desire to be regarded as a useless
fool for Christ, who before me was regarded as such,
rather than as a wise or prudent person in this world.[7]

This kind of humility is not easy for any of us. It seems
weak and foolish, even humiliating, because it runs counter
to all the self-protective and self-promoting inclinations of
our own egos. It also runs counter to the message we are
constantly getting from what Buechner calls "the great blaring, boring, banal voice of mass culture," which, he says,
"threatens to deafen us all by blasting forth that the only

thing that really matters about your work is how much it will get you in the way of salary and status."[8]

Perhaps the best-known modern person whose life has exemplified a radical sense of loving humility was Mother Teresa of Calcutta. Before becoming famous for her work with India's poor, she taught for many years at a missionary high school for girls, mostly from middle-class backgrounds, in Calcutta. During her teaching years, she found herself increasingly disturbed by the sight of the terrible slums and desperately poor people on the streets outside the walls of the convent school compound. Her poignant account of her own call experience captures the moment when she recognized the downward trajectory of her own calling to "be poor with the poor":

> I felt that God wanted from me something more. He wanted me to be poor with the poor and to love him in the distressing disguise of the poorest of the poor. ...It was on the tenth of September 1946, in the train that took me to Darjeeling, the hill station in the Himalayas, that I heard the call of God....The message was quite clear: I was to leave the convent and help the poor whilst living among them.[9]

"Peace of mind" and being "well-adjusted" are also commonly seen as indicators of success or achievement. Superficial contentment and freedom from anxiety, however, do not equate with a "still and quiet conscience," because these things can also be symptoms of spiritual numbness and complacency. A discerning attitude is called for: "Peace of mind," says Sanford, "...may amount to nothing more than an anesthetization of the individual's higher sensibilities....Truly great people have never had much peace of mind, for they were too aware of their own inner conflicts, of the pain and suffering around them, and of their own calling to a life of struggle."[10]

Mother Teresa's peace of mind was disturbed by the human misery around her. It bothered her; she couldn't seem to screen it out or forget it. She experienced, perhaps, something like what Niebuhr called "the agonized conscience of the awakened." In her response to her call, however, she became a living model of what it is like to live with a "consoled conscience," of "one who in the company of the Spirit seeks to fulfill the infinite demands of the infinite other." In her case, the "infinite other" was encountered in the "distressing disguise of the poorest of the poor."

What it means to be a well-adjusted member of society is also a complex matter. It depends, perhaps, on the nature of the particular "status quo" to which one is trying to adjust. Discerning judgments about whether a person is adjusted or maladjusted must take into consideration the moral health and integrity of the social context in which he or she is living. "Adaptation as a standard of wholeness is misleading," says Sanford, "if it is the society in which a person lives that measures the adaptation. If the individual adapts to a sick situation, he [or she] becomes a part of that sickness."[11]

It is hazardous to our moral and spiritual health to allow ourselves to become too comfortable with an unjust status quo. The danger is that we will become successful persons but not "great" persons. "Greatness," says Cornel West, "is telling the truth and being courageous in pursuit of justice. The worst thing you can tell young people is to be successful but become well-adjusted to an unjust status quo, as opposed to being great and being maladjusted to an unjust status quo."[12] Injustice *should* make us uneasy, uncomfortable, sad, ashamed, angry; such feelings are indicators that our consciences are in good working order.

There is also the danger that our lives may show all the outward signs of having "made it," but that we might fail on the inner level of the spirit or on the level of social responsibility, which, in these matters, are hard to separate. "For what shall it profit us if we gain the whole world but lose our own soul?"[13]

Sadly, our success sometimes comes at the *expense* of others. "The nervous, uphill financial climb of the professional middle class," says Barbara Ehrenreich, "accelerates the downward spiral of the society as a whole: toward cruelly widening inequalities, toward heightened estrangement along lines of class and race, and toward the moral anesthesia that estrangement requires."[14] As we become estranged from the poor and the different, we become estranged from our own consciences. The saying, "Live simply, so that others may simply live," implies that if we *don't* live simply and generously, others may have a harder time making it, or perhaps not even be able to make it at all. For example, people in Latin America with families to support are making three dollars a day picking the beans used to make fancy cups of coffee for North Americans. Some of the coffees cost more than what the coffee pickers are paid for a full day's work.

Paradoxically, when we are living in good conscience and doing our best to be faithful to our callings, success and money may sometimes come our way, especially when we are not worried too much about them. I have a vivid memory of an experience at a time in my life when I was very unhappy with a job, but also very worried that I might not be able to earn enough money if I did what I really wanted to do— which was to quit the job and strike out on my own as a self-employed therapist and teacher. One day, feeling depressed and anxious about my dilemma, I boarded a city bus, and, looking up, noticed the title of a book the person sitting across from me happened to be reading: *Do What You Love, The Money Will Follow*.[15] The Voice could not have spoken more loudly and clearly! I eventually made the move I needed to make and was much happier. A lot of money didn't follow, but just enough came in to get along just fine.

Psychiatrist Victor Frankl, who during his stay at Auschwitz learned some hard lessons about what makes for a successful human being, offered this advice to his students:

> Don't aim at success—the more you aim at it and make it a target, the more you are going to miss it. For success, like happiness, cannot be pursued; it must ensue, and it only does so as the unintended side-effect of one's personal dedication to a cause greater than oneself or as the by-product of one's surrender to a person other than oneself. I want you to listen to what your conscience commands you to do and carry it out to the best of your knowledge. Then you will live to see that in the long run—in the long run, I say!—success will follow you precisely because you had *forgotten* to think about it.[16]

In the end, it is very difficult for us to accurately judge the worthiness or success of our own lives. What seems important to us right now may not, in fact, be all that significant in the ultimate scheme of things. On the other hand, what we see as "failure" may look very different in the eyes of God. In the classic Christmas movie "It's a Wonderful Life," George Bailey, the main character, is in suicidal despair over money problems and seeming failures in his life and work. Clarence, the angel, has the mission of helping George remember what really counts: all of the ways his sense of kindness and decency and fairness have made a difference for the better in the lives of the people of his community.

RISKS AND MISTAKES

Sooner or later, after all our imperfect efforts at listening and discerning, there comes a time to make decisions. The challenge then is to make intelligent and courageous choices to *follow* where we are being called or led.

We have a choice about whether to say "yes" or "no" to calls. The stakes are high, and there are risks and consequences either way we go. If we do what we love, there are no guarantees that money will follow, that things will work out according to plan, that we won't get hurt, or that we won't come to the realization down the road that our choice was a mistake.

On the other hand, if we play it safe and say "no" to calls, we also open ourselves up to emotional and spiritual risks. There is no shortage of depressed and empty and bitter people who harbor regrets about "the road not taken" earlier in life, who wish they had done things differently. If they had it to do over again, they might wish they had given their heart more of a voice in important choices in love and work. This sad scenario is poignantly described by Buechner in *The Hungering Dark*:

> The world is full of people who seem to have listened to the wrong voice and are now engaged in life-work in which they find no pleasure or purpose and who run the risk of suddenly realizing some day that they have spent the only years they are ever going to get in this world doing something which could not matter less to themselves or to anyone else...work that seems simply irrelevant not only to the great human needs and issues of our time but also to their own need to grow and develop as humans.[17]

Although various criteria for vocational discernment can be helpful in our decision-making, there is no absolute set of guidelines that can guarantee that we will always make the "right" choice. What is required is a willingness to "experi-

ment with truth," to engage in a process of trial-and-error, to
take the risk of making the best choice we can with the
knowledge we have after careful consideration of all the options. As Jung wrote:

> When one follows the path of individuation, when
> one lives one's own life, one must take mistakes into
> the bargain; life would not be complete without
> them. There is no guarantee—not for a single mo-
> ment—that we will not fall into error or stumble
> into deadly peril. We may think there is a sure road.
> But that would be the road of death. Then nothing
> happens any longer—at any rate, not the right things.
> Anyone who takes the sure road is as good as dead.[18]

This is where *faith* comes in. By faith I do not mean cognitive belief in a particular theological idea or creed, but
rather an attitude characterized by a willingness to follow a
calling simply because we believe it is worth the risk, that
certain dreams are worth pursuing *regardless* of how things
turn out. Goethe wrote eloquently of the amazing ways in
which God seems to provide for people who commit themselves to the risky venture of following their callings:

> Until one is committed, there is hesitancy, the chance
> to draw back, always ineffectiveness. Concerning all acts
> of initiative (and creation) there is one elementary
> truth, the ignorance of which kills countless ideas and
> splendid plans: that the moment one definitely com-
> mits oneself, then Providence moves too. All sorts of
> things occur to help one that would never otherwise
> have occurred. A whole stream of events issues from
> the decision, raising in one's favor all manner of un-
> foreseen incidents and meetings and material assistance,
> which [no one] could have dreamed would come

[their] way. Whatever you can do, or dream you can, begin it. Boldness has genius, power and magic in it.[19]

What Goethe admires as courage or "boldness" might seem like foolishness or even craziness to others. We may fear that people will think we are crazy if we follow the inner voice. "Until I heard the voice, I'd never done a crazy thing in my whole life," says Ray Kinsella, the main character in the movie *Field of Dreams*. Working in his Iowa cornfield one day, Ray hears a mysterious voice that tells him: "If you build it, he will come." Understandably puzzled by this experience and its cryptic message, he gradually begins to realize that the voice wants him to build a baseball diamond so that a long-dead baseball player who had been deprived of the chance to finish his career can have the opportunity to come back and play again. Feeling scared and confused by the bizarre turn of his thoughts, Ray begins to doubt his sanity.

When he tells his wife what he has been thinking, she asks, with some dismay, "Are you *actually* thinking of *doing* this?" Ray, sensing that something very deep is at stake, then reminisces sadly about his deceased father: "He must have had dreams, but he never did anything about them. For all I know, maybe he heard voices too, but he never listened to them." Finally, clear that he does not want to reenact his father's pattern in his own life, and resolved to carry through his strange plan to build the baseball diamond, he asks his wife, "Do you think I'm *crazy*?" "Yes," she responds. After a pause, however, she adds, warmly: "But I also think that if you *really* feel you should do this, you should do it."[20]

The moral of the story is not to recommend that we impulsively or recklessly follow any inclination or fantasy that comes into our heads without regard for the consequences. Rather, the point is that there is a kind of crazy logic about vocation that may not always be easy to justify or explain to others, or sometimes even to ourselves. If we do what we really feel we should do, we run the risk of being perceived as crazy or foolish. Following an unconventional calling that others do not understand or approve can be likened to the kind of holy foolishness that "shames the wise":

> Consider your own call, brothers and sisters: not many of you were wise by human standards, not many were powerful, not many were of noble birth. But God chose what is foolish in the world to shame the wise; God chose what is weak in the world to shame the strong; God chose what is low and despised in the world, things that are not, to reduce to nothing things that are.[21]

Most of us, of course, are not called to do foolish things like building baseball diamonds in cornfields or heroic things like leaving everything to serve the poorest of the poor. All of us, though, are called upon to have courage, to take risks, to be heroes in the pursuit of our own callings, however humble they may be. It takes courage to do with our lives something that is *different* from what everybody else is doing, or from what everybody else thinks we should do. It takes courage, in matters big and small, to do not just the easy thing, but the loving thing, the just thing, the decent thing. In our culture, a kind of countercultural heroism is also required even to keep ourselves attuned to the inner voice of conscience, to allow it have a say in our lives, to give the voice its due.

LOVE AND DEATH

"*Carpe diem!*" cries Mr. Keating to his students, "Seize the day!" In the movie *Dead Poets Society*, the teacher, on the first

day of school, has taken the unorthodox approach of reminding his students that, sooner or later, they are all going to die.
He wants to shake them up, to *wake* them up, in the hope
that they will make the most of their lives before it is too late,
before they are dead: "Make your lives extraordinary!"

Perhaps one of our greatest fears is the prospect of reaching the end of our lives only to discover, with regret, that we
failed to make the most of the time we had on this earth, that
we did not "seize the day" when we had the opportunity. On
some level of our souls, all of us share the concern that drove
Thoreau into the woods near Walden Pond: "I went to the
woods," he wrote, "because I wished to live deliberately, to
front only the essential facts of life, and see if I could not
learn what it had to teach, and not, when I came to die, discover that I had not lived."[22]

The disconcerting fact of our own mortality is one of the
"essential facts of life." The emotional and spiritual challenge
is to allow the awareness of our mortality into our consciousness so that we can find out what it has to teach us. The
learning process requires a willingness to let death "work" on
us, to allow ourselves to feel its repercussions in our souls, its
implications for how we should live our lives. In *The Saints'
Guide to Happiness,* Robert Ellsberg discusses the transformative potential of this kind of contemplation:

> The contemplation of death, up close, does not sup-
> ply new information so much as a new vantage
> point. The world looks different from there. This
> change of standpoint can be an occasion of fear,
> depression, and horror. We may be confronted by
> how unprepared we are, by the many things we
> wish we had done differently, by so much we have
> left unfinished or unresolved. But the approach of
> death, it is said, can also have a strangely liberating
> effect. Many people testify that they never felt so

fully alive as when facing the prospect of death. So many cares and worries became irrelevant. So many things were clarified and revealed according to their true value.[23]

Remembering death helps us to get our priorities straight; it has the potential to clarify and reveal things "according to their true value." In such moments of clarity we can tell the difference between what is relevant—and therefore worthy of our attention—and what should be ignored. We are able to recognize what is most important and distinguish it from what is less important, or from what is not really important at all. We remember, at least for the moment, what is worth living for, striving for, sacrificing for—perhaps even *dying* for: "There are some things so dear," said Martin Luther King Jr., "some things so precious, some things so eternally true, that they're worth dying for."[24]

People in extreme circumstances are sometimes better able to appreciate the things that are most important. In the loveless environment of the Auschwitz death camp, Victor Frankl came to the realization that what is ultimately most dear and precious and eternally true is *love*:

A thought transfixed me: for the first time in my life I saw the truth as it is set into song by so many poets, proclaimed as the final wisdom by so many thinkers. The truth—that love is the ultimate and the highest goal to which we can aspire. Then I grasped the meaning of the greatest secret that human poetry and human thought and belief have to impart: *The salvation of humanity is through love and in love.*[25]

Frankl, a Jewish psychiatrist, poignantly reminds us of the universal truth at the heart of all authentic religion: only *love* can save us.

On the theme of "salvation through love and in love," there is a passage from Matthew's gospel that has haunted and inspired Christians to loving service and action for two thousand years. The story of the "Last Judgment" suggests that, in the mind of Jesus, our lives are ultimately evaluated or judged by a simple standard: whether or not we have been loving persons during our lifetime. Mysteriously, Jesus goes so far as to say that it is *he* we encounter in human beings who are suffering or in need, *he* whose needs are either attended or neglected in our dealings with those whose pain or plight calls for a compassionate response from us:

> I was hungry and you gave me food; I was thirsty and you gave me something to drink; I was a stranger and you welcomed me; I was naked and you gave me clothing; I was sick and you took care of me; I was in prison and you visited me.... Truly I tell you, just as you did it to one of the least of these who are members of my family, you did it to me.[26]

Just a few months before his assassination, Martin Luther King Jr.—who himself seemed haunted by these words of Jesus—gave a speech in which he shared his thoughts about what he would want to be said about his life after he was gone: "Now and then," he said, "I think about my own death and my own funeral, and I ask myself, 'What would I want said?'" He made clear that he did *not* want the externals, what he called the "shallow things of life," to be emphasized (his Nobel Peace Prize, where he went to school, etc.). Instead, he wanted his life to be remembered for other things:

> I'd like somebody to mention that day that Martin Luther King, Jr., tried to give his life serving others. I'd like for somebody to say that day that Martin

Luther King, Jr., tried to *love* somebody. . . . I want you to be able to say that day that I *did* try to feed the hungry . . . to clothe those who were naked . . . to visit those who were in prison . . . I want you to say that I tried to be right on the war question. I want you to say that I tried to love and serve humanity. . . . And all of the other shallow things will not matter. I won't have any money to leave behind. I won't have the fine and luxurious things of life to leave behind. But I just want to leave a committed life behind.[27]

HOW CAN I KEEP FROM SINGING?

Sadly, according to Thoreau, most people "lead lives of quiet desperation and go to the grave with the song still in them."[28] They cannot hear "the singing underneath," or perhaps are too inhibited to sing their song while they have the chance.[29] So many things hold us back from pursuing our dreams. Still, there is a yearning in all of us to let the song out, to sing it before we die: "*Y antes de morir, me quiero echar mis versos del alma*" ("And before dying, I want to share these poems of my soul").[30]

Metaphors of music and song are natural and fitting for putting mysterious and intangible matters of vocation into words. We speak of being in tune or in synch with the rhythm or melody of the soul, of "marching to a different drummer." The title of a book on the art of discernment is *Listening to the Music of the Spirit*.[31] The beautiful old Quaker hymn "How Can I Keep from Singing?" resonates deeply:

My life flows on in endless song above earth's lamentation,

I hear the real, though far off hymn, that hails a new
   creation.

No storm can shake my inmost calm, while to that
   rock I'm clinging,
Since Love is Lord of heaven and earth, how can I
   keep from singing?[32]

The new creation hailed by the "far off hymn" is not just
for the fortunate, privileged few, but for *all* of us. And the
hymn, I think, is not a new-age melody composed only for
the listening pleasure of people who have the luxury of following their bliss. It sounds more like what Gustavo Gutiérrez
calls the "song of the poor,"[33] or, perhaps, like Bob Marley's
"Redemption Song." We are invited not just to listen, but to
join in, to *help* in singing a redemption song:

Won't you help to sing these songs of freedom?
'cause all I ever had: redemption songs, redemption
   songs.[34]

A very beautiful redemption song is heard in the story of
Etty Hillesum, a young Jewish woman from the Netherlands
who was sent, along with her parents and her brother Mischa, to her death at Auschwitz during the Holocaust. On
September 7, 1943, when they were packed into freight cars
on the train bound for Auschwitz, Etty wrote these words to
a friend on a postcard that she threw out of the train:

Opening the Bible at random I find this: "The Lord
is my high tower." I am sitting on a rucksack in the
middle of a full freight car. Father, Mother, and Mischa are a few cars away. In the end, the departure
came without warning. On special orders from the
Hague. We left the camp singing, Father and Mother

firmly and calmly, Mischa too. We shall be traveling for three days . . .[35]

"We left the camp singing." May all of us sing so bravely and firmly and calmly when we are called upon to do so! And may all of us be so brave and firm and calm in following our consciences and our callings in matters big and small. A prayer from Etty Hillesum's diary is a fitting conclusion to this book:

Oh God, I thank you for having created me as I am. I thank you for the sense of fulfillment I sometimes have: that fulfillment is after all nothing but being filled with You. I promise You to strive my whole life long for beauty and harmony and also humility and true love, whispers of which I hear inside me during my best moments.[36]

NOTES

PREFACE

1. Mary Oliver, "The Summer Day," *New and Selected Poems* (Boston, MA: Beacon Press, 1992).

2. See Thomas Merton's reflections on vocation and salvation in his chapter "Vocation and Modern Thought," in *Contemplation in a World of Action* (Notre Dame, IN: University of Notre Dame Press, 1998). Also see his essay "Learning to Live," in *Love and Living* (1965; New York: Bantam Books, 1979).

3. Ezekiel 11:19.

4. *The Call of Conscience* is the title of a recent collection of the speeches of Dr. Martin Luther King Jr. edited by C. Carson and K. Shepard (New York: Warner Books, 2001).

5. John G. Neihardt, *Black Elk Speaks: Being the Life Story of a Holy Man of the Oglala Sioux* (Lincoln, NE: University of Nebraska Press, 1932), 19.

6. The original photo, part of a series of four titled "Esclarecimiento," appeared on the cover of the fourth volume of the REHMI report, *Guatemala Nunca Mas: Victimas del Conflicto* (Oficina de Derechos Humanos del Arzobispado de Guatemala, Informe Projecto Interdiocesano de Recuperacion de la Memoria Historica, 1998). Together, all four photos can be seen on the cover of the English language version of the REHMI report, *Guatemala Never Again! The Official Report of the Human Rights Office, Archdiocese of Guatemala* (Maryknoll, NY: Orbis Books, 1999).

7. William Butler Yeats, "A Drinking Song," *The Collected Poems of W. B. Yeats,* ed. Richard J. Finneran (1921; New York: Collier Books, 1989), 93.

1. INTRODUCTION

1. Frederick Buechner, *Wishful Thinking: A Seeker's ABC* (1973; San Francisco: HarperSanFrancisco, 1993), 119.

2. Mohandas K. Gandhi, *Collected Works*, LV:255. Originally published in Gandhi's journal, *Harijan,* July 8, 1933.

3. José A. Garcia, S.J., "The School of the Heart," *The Way* 42, no. 2 (April 2003): 10.

4. Evelyn and James Whitehead, *Seasons of Strength: New Visions of Adult Christian Maturing* (Garden City, NY: Doubleday & Company, 1984), 10.

5. James Hillman, *The Soul's Code: In Search of Character and Calling* (New York: Random House, 1996), 252.

6. Micah 6:8.

7. C. G. Jung, *The Development of Personality* (New York: Bollingen Foundation, 1954), 176.

8. Thomas Kelly, *A Testament of Devotion* (San Francisco: HarperSanFrancisco, 1992), 3.

9. Laurence G. Boldt, *How to Find the Work You Love* (New York: Penguin Arkana, 1996), 25.

10. See C. G. Jung, *Memories, Dreams, and Reflections* (New York: Vintage Books, 1965). Jung was strongly influenced by the thinking of the German theologian Rudolph Otto on the sacred or "numinous" dimension of human experience. See Otto's classic book *The Idea of the Holy* (London: Oxford University Press, 1923).

11. Jung, *Memories, Dreams, and Reflections.*

12. Edward C. Whitmont, *Return of the Goddess* (New York: Crossroad, 1984), 206.

13. See Merton's essay "Final Integration: Toward a 'Monastic Therapy,'" in *Contemplation in a World of Action* (1971; Notre Dame, IN: University of Notre Dame Press, 1998), 201–2.

14. See Russell B. Connors Jr. and Patrick T. McCormick, *Character, Choices, and Community: The Three Faces of Christian Ethics* (Mahwah, NJ: Paulist Press, 1998), 138.

15. Mohandas K. Gandhi, *The Way to God,* ed. M. S. Desphande (Berkeley, CA: Berkeley Hills Books, 1999), 96–97. Originally published in *Harijan,* July 8, 1933.

16. William James, *The Varieties of Religious Experience* (1902; New York: Simon & Schuster, 1997), 62.

17. Matthew 13:14–15. Jesus is referring to Isaiah 6:9–10.

18. William Least Heat Moon, *Blue Highways: A Journey into America* (New York: Fawcett Crest, 1982), 17.

19. Saint Ignatius used the words *scuela del affecto*. See Garcia, "The School of the Heart," 4–15. Also see William Barry, S.J., *Spiritual Direction and the Encounter with God* (Mahwah, NJ: Paulist Press, 1992), 82–83.

20. See Shunryu Suzuki, *Zen Mind, Beginner's Mind* (New York: John Weatherhill, Inc., 1970).

21. Isaiah 50:4–5.

22. Etty Hillesum, *An Interrupted Life and Letters from Westerbork* (New York: Henry Holt and Company, 1996), 183.

23. Eduardo Galeano, "Celebration of the Human Voice," *The Book of Embraces* (New York: W. W. Norton, 1991), 25.

24. Wilson Van Dusen, *The Natural Depth in Man* (New York: Swedenborg Foundation, Inc., 1972), 18.

25. Daniel Hartnett, S.J., "The Heuristics of Justice," *Proceedings of the 65th Annual Meeting of the Jesuit Philosophical Association* (2004).

26. Thomas Merton, *Love and Living* (1965; New York: Bantam Books, 1979), 3.

27. Psalm 25:4–5.

28. The story of the rich young man can be found in Mark 10:17–22 (parallels in Matthew 19:16–22; Luke 18:18–23).

29. Walter Brueggemann, "Covenanting as Human Vocation: A Discussion of the Relation of Bible and Pastoral Care," *Interpretation* 33, no. 2 (1979): 115–29.

30. William Barry has referred to this state of affairs as being "out of tune with the action or intention of God." See Barry, *Spiritual Direction and the Encounter with God*, 76.

31. John A. Sanford, *Healing Body and Soul: The Meaning of Illness in the New Testament and in Psychotherapy* (Louisville, KY: Westminster/John Knox, 1992), 6.

32. It is important to make a distinction between egocentrism and healthy forms of self-care or self-interest.

33. John A. Sanford, *The Man Who Wrestled with God: Light from*

the Old Testament on the Psychology of Individuation (Mahwah, NJ: Paulist Press, 1981), 21.

34. Luke 22:42; Matthew 26:39; Mark 14:36.

35. Merton, *Love and Living*, 4.

36. John de Graaf, David Wann, and Thomas H. Naylor, *Affluenza: The All-Consuming Epidemic* (San Francisco: Berrett-Koehler Publishers, 2001), 2.

37. Thomas Groome, *Educating for Life: A Spiritual Vision for Every Teacher and Parent* (New York: Crossroad, 1998), 36.

38. Sharon Daloz Parks, *Big Questions, Worthy Dreams* (San Francisco: Jossey-Bass, 2000), 152 (emphasis mine).

39. Thomas Moore, *The Education of the Heart* (New York: HarperCollins Publishers, 1996), 3.

40. Merton, *Love and Living,* 4.

2. SACRED VOICES

1. Jon Sobrino, *Where Is God? Earthquake, Terrorism, Barbarity, and Hope* (Maryknoll, NY: Orbis Books, 2004), 45.

2. Mark 4:9; Matthew 13:9; Luke 8:8 (emphasis mine).

3. "I hear it in the deep heart's core" is the last line of Yeats's poem "The Lake Isle of Innisfree." See *The Collected Poems of W. B. Yeats,* ed. Richard J. Finneran (1921; New York: Collier Books, 1989), 39.

4. Marcus Borg, *Meeting Jesus Again for the First Time* (San Francisco: HarperSanFrancisco, 1994), 32–33.

5. Exodus 3:4.

6. Mark 1:9–11; parallels in Luke 3:21–22 and Matthew 3:13–17.

7. *Hadith*, Volume 1, Book 1, Number 3.

8. John A. Sanford, *The Man Who Wrestled with God: Light from the Old Testament on the Psychology of Individuation* (Mahwah, NJ: Paulist Press, 1981), 84.

9. Quoted in John A. Sanford, *Healing and Wholeness* (Mahwah, NJ: Paulist Press, 1977), 68.

10. As narrated to John G. Neihardt, *Black Elk Speaks: Being the Life Story of a Holy Man of the Oglala Sioux* (Lincoln, NE: University of Nebraska Press, 1932), 19.

11. Neihardt, *Black Elk Speaks,* 204–5.

12. Karen Armstrong, *Muhammad: A Biography of the Prophet* (San Francisco: HarperSanFrancisco, 1992). See especially chapter 4, "Revelation," 72–90.

13. The story of Jacob and the angel can be found in Genesis 32:24–32.

14. *Hadith,* Volume 1, Book 1, Number 3. This is the account of Muhammad's calling as remembered by his wife A'isha.

15. Margaret Guenther, *The Practice of Prayer* (New York: Cowley, 1998), 36.

16. Hebrews 13:2.

17. This poem is known as the "Celtic Rune of Hospitality."

18. For a thorough recent analysis of the staggering problem of global poverty, see Jeffrey D. Sachs, *The End of Poverty: Economic Possibilities for Our Time* (New York: Penguin, 2005).

19. Leonardo and Clodovis Boff, *Introducing Liberation Theology* (Maryknoll, NY: Orbis Books, 2004), 31.

20. Cornel West, *Prophetic Thought in Postmodern Times* (Monroe, ME: Common Courage Press, 1993), 4.

21. Frantz Fanon, *The Wretched of the Earth* (New York: Grove Press, 1963).

22. Nelson Maldonado Torres, "The Cry of the Self as the Call from the Other: The Paradoxical Loving Subjectivity of Frantz Fanon," *Listening: The Journal of Religion and Culture* 36, no. 1 (Winter 2001): 46–60.

23. Exodus 2:23–24.

24. Exodus 3:7–10.

25. See Jon Sobrino's chapter "Human Rights and Oppressed Peoples: Historical-Theological Reflections," in *Truth and Memory: The Church and Human Rights in El Salvador and Guatemala,* ed. M. A. Hayes and D. Tombs (London: Gracewing, 2001), 134–58.

26. Paul Farmer, *Pathologies of Power: Health, Human Rights, and the New War on the Poor* (Berkeley, CA: University of California Press, 2003). Farmer's personal story is told in a recent biography by Tracy Kidder, *Mountains Beyond Mountains: The Quest of Dr. Paul Farmer, A Man Who Would Cure the World* (New York: Random House, 2004).

27. Dean Brackley, S.J., "Meeting the Victims, Falling in Love," originally published in *Salvanet*, a publication of Christians for Peace in El Salvador, CRISPAZ, January/February 2000.

28. 1 Kings 19:9–13 (Revised Standard Version).

29. See Robert Ellsberg's chapter "Learning to Sit Still," in *The Saints' Guide to Happiness* (New York: North Point Press, 2003).

30. James Hillman, *Insearch: Psychology and Religion* (1967; Woodstock, CT: Spring Publications, 1994), 21.

31. Margaret Guenther, *The Practice of Prayer* (New York: Cowley, 1998), 39.

32. John Boyle O'Reilly, "The Cry of the Dreamer," in A. G. Evans, *Fanatic Heart: A Life of John Boyle O'Reilly*, 1844–1890 (Boston: Northeastern University Press, 1997), 233–34.

33. Friedrich Heiler, *Prayer: A Study in the History and Psychology of Religion* (Oxford, England: Oneworld Publications, 1932), 356.

34. John A. Sanford, *Healing Body and Soul: The Meaning of Illness in the New Testament and in Psychotherapy* (Louisville, KY: Westminster/John Knox Press, 1992), 86–87.

35. Ibid., 87.

36. Robert Ochs, *God Is More Present than You Think* (Mahwah, NJ: Paulist Press, 1973).

37. Henri Nouwen, *Life of the Beloved: Spiritual Living in a Secular World* (New York: Crossroad, 1992).

38. See Mark 1:11 and parallels in Luke 3:22 and Matthew 3:17. Interestingly, in Mark and Luke the voice is addressed *personally* to Jesus and says: "*You* are my beloved Son; with whom I am well pleased," suggesting that Jesus may have experienced it privately as an *inner* voice. In Matthew, the voice is described as a kind of public announcement to the crowd gathered at the Jordan River, saying "*This* is my beloved son…"

39. Nouwen, *Life of the Beloved,* 62–63.

3. DISCERNMENT

1. Michael J. Himes, *Doing the Truth in Love: Conversations about God, Relationships, and Service* (Mahwah, NJ: Paulist Press, 1995), 55.

2. Frederick Buechner, *Wishful Thinking: A Theological ABC* (1973; San Francisco: HarperSanFrancisco, 1993), 118.

3. James Joyce, *A Portrait of the Artist as a Young Man* (1916; London: Granada Publishing, 1977), 154.

4. From William H. Sheldon, *Psychology and the Promethean Will.* Quoted in *The Choice Is Always Ours,* ed. D. B. Phillips, E. B. Howes, and L. M. Nixon (Wheaton, IL: Re-Quest Books, 1982), 33–34.

5. C. G. Jung, *Memories, Dreams, and Reflections* (New York: Vintage Books, 1965), 199.

6. This is the central image in a book on Ignatian spirituality by Margaret Silf, *The Inner Compass: An Invitation to Ignatian Spirituality* (Chicago, IL: Loyola Press, 1999).

7. David Lonsdale, S.J., *Listening to the Music of the Spirit: The Art of Discernment* (Notre Dame, IN: Ave Maria Press, 1992), 72–73.

8. For an excellent cross-cultural overview of shamanic beliefs from an anthropological perspective, see David Kinsley, *Health, Healing, and Religion: A Cross-Cultural Perspective* (Upper Saddle River, NJ: Prentice-Hall, 1996).

9. Nikos Kazantzakis, *The Last Temptation of Christ* (New York: Simon & Schuster, 1960), 15.

10. David Fleming, S.J., *Spiritual Exercises of St. Ignatius: A Literal Translation and a Contemporary Reading* (St. Louis: Institute of Jesuit Sources, 1978), 202.

11. Here again it is important to make a distinction between egocentrism and emotionally and spiritually healthy forms of self-care or self-interest.

12. Iris Murdoch, *The Black Prince* (1973; New York, Penguin Books, 1975), 183.

13. According to James Neafsey (personal communication): "'God-centered inclinations' are also 'other-centered.' That is, impulses to genuine love may be for *someone* [i.e., another human person] as well as toward God *in* and *through* that someone. Ignatius doesn't say it this way exactly, but many movements of the Spirit don't immediately appear to have God as their direct orientation (though God may inspire the love and ultimately be the object of the love)."

14. Himes, *Doing the Truth in Love.* See especially the section on "Discerning Our Call to Serve," 55–59.

15. Ibid., 57.

16. According to Saint Paul, "the fruit of the Spirit is love, joy, peace, patience, kindness, generosity, faithfulness, gentleness, and self-control" (Galatians 5:22–23).

17. See especially the chapter "Convalescence and Conversion," in *The Autobiography of Saint Ignatius Loyola*, ed. John Olin, trans. Joseph O'Callaghan (New York: Fordham University Press, 1992), 21–28.

18. Sam Keen, *Hymns to an Unknown God* (New York: Bantam, 1994), 279.

19. 1 Corinthians 12:4–7.

20. Keen, *Hymns to an Unknown God*, 279.

21. Himes, *Doing the Truth in Love*, 58.

22. Frederick Buechner, *The Hungering Dark* (San Francisco: Harper & Row, 1985), 29.

23. Daniel Hartnett, S.J., "The Heuristics of Justice," *Proceedings of the 65th Annual Meeting of the Jesuit Philosophical Association* (2004), 10.

24. Joe Holland and Peter Henriot, *Social Analysis: Linking Faith and Justice* (Maryknoll, NY: Orbis Books, 1983).

25. Hartnett, "The Heuristics of Justice," 9.

26. Paolo Freire, *Pedagogy of the Oppressed* (1970; New York: Continuum, 1996), 17.

27. Leonardo Boff, *Faith on the Edge: Religion and Marginalized Existence* (San Francisco: Harper and Row, 1989), 23.

28. Dr. Paul Farmer provides a thoughtful review of this methodology in his chapter "Health, Healing, and Social Justice: Insights from Liberation Theology," in *Pathologies of Power: Health, Human Rights, and the New War on the Poor* (Berkeley, CA: University of California Press, 2003), 139–59.

29. Farmer, *Pathologies of Power*, 142.

30. Desmond Tutu, *God Has a Dream* (New York: Doubleday, 2004), 40.

31. Mary Elizabeth Hobgood, *Dismantling Privilege: An Ethics of Accountability* (Cleveland, OH: Pilgrim Press, 2000), 25.

32. Luke 12:48.

33. See Brueggemann's chapter "Voices of the Night—Against Justice," in Walter Brueggemann, Sharon Daloz Parks, and Thomas

H. Groome, *Act Justly, Love Tenderly, Walk Humbly: An Agenda for Ministers* (Eugene, OR: Wipf & Stock Publishers, 1997), 5.

34. Farmer, *Pathologies of Power,* 138.

35. *Mohandas Gandhi: Essential Writings,* ed. John Dear (Maryknoll, NY: Orbis Books, 2002), 190–91.

4. AUTHENTICITY

1. Parker Palmer, *Let Your Life Speak: Listening for the Voice of Vocation* (San Francisco: Jossey-Bass, 2000), 16.

2. From Bishop Juan Gerardi's speech on the occasion of the presentation of the findings of the REHMI (Recuperation of Historical Memory Project) report in the Metropolitan Cathedral of Guatemala City, April 24, 1998. *Guatemala Never Again! The Official Report of Human Rights Office, Archdiocese of Guatemala* (Maryknoll, NY: Orbis Books, 1999), xxiii.

3. William Shakespeare, *Hamlet,* Act I, scene iii.

4. Thomas Merton, *New Seeds of Contemplation* (New York: New Directions, 1962), 31.

5. See "Ego Distortion in Terms of True and False Self," in D. W. Winnicott, *The Maturational Processes and the Facilitating Environment* (New York: International Universities Press, 1965).

6. William James, *The Varieties of Religious Experience* (1902; New York: Simon & Schuster, 1997), 398.

7. *The Letters of William James*, ed. Henry James (Boston: The Atlantic Monthly Press, 1920), 199. I have taken the liberty of using non-sexist language in the quotation.

8. Merton, *New Seeds of Contemplation,* 34.

9. John Boyle O'Reilly, "The Cry of the Dreamer," in A. G. Evans, *Fanatic Heart: A Life of John Boyle O'Reilly*, 1844–1890 (Boston: Northeastern University Press, 1997), 233–34.

10. This material is adapted from my chapter "Psychological Dimensions of the Discernment of Vocation," in *Re-Visiting the Idea of Vocation: Theological Explorations,* ed. John Haughey (Washington, DC: Catholic University Press, 2004).

11. Winnicott, "Ego Distortion in Terms of True and False Self."

12. William F. Lynch, *Images of Hope: Imagination as Healer of the Hopeless* (Notre Dame, IN: University of Notre Dame Press, 1965). See especially the chapter entitled "The Science of the Bare Fact."

13. For an interesting application of Winnicott's ideas to the process of psychotherapy, see Alice Miller, *The Drama of the Gifted Child: The Search for the True Self* (New York: Basic Books, 1981).

14. Harry Guntrip, *Psychoanalytic Theory, Therapy, and the Self* (New York: Basic Books, 1971), 182. I have changed the gender pronouns in the original quote from masculine to feminine.

15. William Pollack offers some thoughtful reflections on homosexuality and self-acceptance in *Real Boys: Rescuing Our Sons from the Myths of Boyhood* (New York: Henry Holt & Co., 1998).

16. Mary Pipher examines the emotional dilemmas of adolescent girls in American culture in *Reviving Ophelia: Saving the Selves of Adolescent Girls* (New York: Ballantine Books, 2002).

17. C. G. Jung, "Psychotherapists or the Clergy," in *Modern Man in Search of a Soul* (New York: Harcourt, Brace & World, Inc., 1933), 236.

18. Martin Buber, *Tales of the Hasidim: The Early Masters* (New York: Shocken Books, 1975), 251.

19. Wilkie Au and Noreen Cannon offer a balanced, holistic perspective on holiness and wholeness in *Urgings of the Heart: A Spirituality of Integration* (Mahwah, NJ: Paulist Press, 1999).

20. Luke 6:41–42. John Sanford has written a thoughtful book on the psychological wisdom of Jesus: *The Kingdom Within: The Inner Meaning of Jesus' Sayings* (1970; San Francisco: HarperSan-Francsico, 1987).

21. J. T. Maltsberger and D. H. Buie use this term in their insightful article "Countertransference Hate in the Treatment of Suicidal Patients," *Archives of General Psychiatry* 30 (1974): 625–33.

22. Thich Nhat Hanh, *The Miracle of Mindfulness* (Boston, MA: Beacon Press, 1975), 37.

23. James Hillman, *Insearch: Psychology and Religion* (1967; Woodstock, CT: Spring Publications, 1994), 76.

24. This was the first *satyagraha* vow. *Satyagraha* literally means "holding on to truth."

25. *Mohandas Gandhi: Essential Writings*, ed. John Dear (Maryknoll, NY: Orbis Books, 2002), 104.

26. M. Scott Peck, *People of the Lie: The Hope for Healing Human Evil* (New York: Simon & Schuster, 1983), 218.

27. Maureen Dowd, "Defining Victory Down," *The New York Times*, January 9, 2005.

28. Mark Twain, *The Mysterious Stranger and Other Stories* (1910; New York: Signet Classic, 1962), 239–40.

29. This expression was used in a communication from the Zapatista rebels in southern Mexico to explain the motives for their rebellion. Quoted in Paul Farmer, *Pathologies of Power: Health, Human Rights, and the New War on the Poor* (Berkeley, CA: University of California Press, 2003), 145.

30. James Carroll, "The Bushes' New World Disorder," *Boston Globe*, March 16, 2004.

31. Susan Sontag, "Regarding the Torture of Others," *The New York Times*, May 23, 2004.

32. Sontag refers to this quote from Secretary of Defense Donald Rumsfeld in her essay.

33. Jeremiah 6:10, 14–15.

34. William Sloane Coffin, *Passion for the Possible: A Message to U.S. Churches*, 2nd ed. (Louisville, KY: Westminster/John Knox Press, 2004), 50.

35. "Civilian Toll in Iraq Is Placed at Nearly 25,000," *The New York Times*, July 20, 2005. Other estimates of civilian casualties have run as high as one hundred thousand.

36. Robert Jay Lifton, "Conditions of Atrocity," *The Nation*, May 31, 2004.

37. From the title song of the Bruce Springsteen CD "Devils and Dust" (Sony, 2005).

38. See, for example, Mark Danner, *Torture and Truth: America, Abu Ghraib, and the War on Terror* (New York: New York Review of Books, 2004).

39. Dean Brackley, S.J., "Meeting the Victims, Falling in Love," originally published in *Salvanet*, a publication of Christians for Peace in El Salvador, CRISPAZ, January/February 2000.

40. John 8:31.

41. The phrase "doing the truth" comes from Enda McDonagh, *Doing the Truth: The Quest for Moral Theology* (Notre Dame, IN: University of Notre Dame Press, 1979).

42. Michael Himes, *Doing the Truth in Love: Conversations about God, Relationships, and Service* (Mahwah, NJ: Paulist Press, 1995).

43. Russell B. Connors Jr. and Patrick T. McCormick, *Character, Choices, and Community: The Three Faces of Christian Ethics* (Mahwah, NJ: Paulist Press, 1998), 115.

44. From Berrigan's introduction to Dorothy Day's autobiography, *The Long Loneliness* (1954; San Francisco: Harper and Row, 1981), xxii–xxiii.

45. The entire text of Bishop Gerardi's speech can be found in *Guatemala Never Again!*, xxiii–xxv.

46. From James Russell Lowell's poem, "The Present Crisis" (1844).

5. PASSION AND COMPASSION

1. E. Edward Kinerk, S.J., "Eliciting Great Desires: Their Place in the Spirituality of the Society of Jesus," *Studies in the Spirituality of Jesuits* 16, no. 5 (November 1984): 1–34.

2. Walter Brueggemann, "Covenanting as Human Vocation: A Discussion of the Relation of Bible and Pastoral Care," *Interpretation* 33, no. 2 (1979): 115–29.

3. Blaise Pascal, *Pensées,* 474. English translation of original Pascal quote by John S. Dunne in *The Reasons of the Heart* (Notre Dame, IN: University of Notre Dame Press, 1978), xii.

4. Martin Buber, *The Way of Man According to the Teaching of Hasidism* (Secaucus, NJ: The Citadel Press, 1966), 15.

5. James Hillman, *Insearch: Psychology and Religion* (1967; Woodstock, CT: Spring Publications, 1994), 66–67.

6. See "Sacrifice and Bliss" chapter in Joseph Campbell (with Bill Moyers), *The Power of Myth* (New York: Doubleday, 1988), 147.

7. Edward C. Whitmont, *Return of the Goddess* (New York: Crossroad, 1984), 223.

8. John S. Dunne, *The Reasons of the Heart* (Notre Dame, IN: University of Notre Dame Press, 1978), xii.

9. Michael J. O'Sullivan, S.J., "Trust Your Feelings but Use Your Head," *Studies in the Spirituality of Jesuits* 22, no. 4 (September 1990): 36.

10. James Joyce, *A Portrait of the Artist as a Young Man* (1916; London: Granada Publishing, 1977), 156.

11. Frederick Buechner, *The Sacred Journey: A Memoir of Early Days* (San Francisco: HarperSanFrancisco, 1982), 52. William Barry reflects on the religious dimensions of this passage from Buechner in *Spiritual Direction and the Encounter with God* (Mahwah, NJ: Paulist Press, 1992).

12. Stanley Greenspan (with Nancy Breslau Lewis), *Building Healthy Minds: Six Experiences That Create Intelligence and Emotional Growth in Babies and Young Children* (New York: Da Capo Press, 1999), 54–55.

13. This saying is attributed to Fr. Pedro Arrupe, S.J. (1907–1991), superior general of the Society of Jesus (the Jesuits) from 1961 to 1984.

14. Michael J. Himes, *Doing the Truth in Love: Conversations about God, Relationships, and Service* (Mahwah, NJ: Paulist Press, 1995), 56.

15. See 1 John 3:20.

16. James Fowler, *Weaving the New Creation: Stages of Faith and the Public Church* (San Francisco: HarperSanFrancisco, 1991), 123.

17. Kinerk, "Eliciting Great Desires," 134.

18. C. S. Lewis, *The Weight of Glory* (1965; San Francisco: HarperSanFrancisco, 2001), 26.

19. Thomas Merton, *The Wisdom of the Desert* (Boston, MA: Shambhala, 1970), 106.

20. Josephine Baker is quoted in James Hillman, *The Soul's Code: In Search of Character and Calling* (New York: Random House, 1996), xii.

21. This phrase is used by Dallas Willard in *Hearing God: Developing a Conversational Relationship with God* (Downers Grove, IL: InterVarsity Press, 1999).

22. Luke 24:32.

23. Kinerk, "Eliciting Great Desires," 4.

24. Quotation from Cesar Chavez in Frederick John Dalton, *The Moral Vision of Cesar Chavez* (Maryknoll, NY: Orbis Books, 2003), 162.

25. *The American Heritage Dictionary*.

26. John G. Neihardt, *Black Elk Speaks: Being the Life Story of a Holy Man of the Oglala Sioux* (Lincoln, NE: University of Nebraska Press, 1932), 200–2.

27. Mark 1:40–41 (emphasis mine).

28. December 6, 1906, letter from Sigmund Freud to C. G. Jung, *The Freud/Jung Letters,* ed. William McGuire (1974; Cambridge, MA: Harvard University Press, 1988), 12–13.

29. Ezekiel 11:19.

30. Walter Brueggemann, *The Prophetic Imagination* (1978; Minneapolis, MN: Fortress Press, 2001).

31. Cornel West, *Democracy Matters: Winning the Fight Against Imperialism* (New York: Penguin, 2004), 214–15.

32. Jeremiah 8:21–9:1.

33. Rother's story can be found in *Love in a Fearful Land: A Guatemalan Story,* by Henri J. M. Nouwen (Notre Dame, IN: Ave Maria Press, 1985). Also see *The Shepherd Will Not Run: Letters of Stanley Rother, Missionary and Martyr* (Archdiocese of Oklahoma City, 1984) and D. W. and E. T. Brett, *Murdered in Central America* (Maryknoll, NY: Orbis Books, 1988).

34. Renny Golden, "The Gringo's Heart," *The Hour of the Furnaces* (Minneapolis: MN: Mid-List Press, 2000).

6. VISION

1. John Boyle O'Reilly, "The Cry of the Dreamer," in A. G. Evans, *Fanatic Heart: A Life of John Boyle O'Reilly, 1844–1890* (Boston: Northeastern University Press, 1997), 233–34.

2. See Joseph Epes Brown, *The Sacred Pipe: Black Elk's Account of the Seven Sacred Rites of the Oglala Sioux* (1953; New York, Penguin Books, 1971).

3. John Lame Deer, in Richard Erdoes, *Crying for a Dream* (Santa Fe, NM: Bear & Company, 1990), 28.

4. Daine-Marie Blinn, Ph.D., Teacher's Guide to *Vision Quest: Men, Women, and Sacred Sites of the Sioux Nation,* CD-ROM by Don Doll, S.J. Teacher's Guide copyright September 1996 by Diane-Marie Blinn.

5. Quotation from Leonard Crow Dog in Joan Halifax, *Shamanic Voices: A Survey of Visionary Narratives* (New York: Arkana, 1979), 85.

6. See John A. Sanford, *Dreams: God's Forgotten Language* (1968; San Francisco: HarperSanFrancisco, 1989).

7. Brown, *The Sacred Pipe,* 59.

8. Quoted in John A. Sanford, *Dreams and Healing* (New York: Paulist Press, 1978). Original quote from *The Religion of Lincoln,* by William J. Wolf (New York: Seabury Press, 1963), 29.

9. Numbers 12:6. A review of all references to dreams in the Bible can be found in Morton T. Kelsey, *God, Dreams, and Revelation* (1968; Minneapolis, MN: Augsburg, 1991).

10. Job 4:12–17 and 33:14–16.

11. Dream passages are found in Matthew 1:20–21; Matthew 2:12; Matthew 2:13; Matthew 2:19–20; and Matthew 2:22.

12. Daniel 2:30 (emphasis mine). Sanford explores this passage in depth in *Dreams and Healing,* 12–15.

13. Sanford, *Dreams and Healing,* 5.

14. 1 Samuel 3:8–9.

15. Henry David Thoreau, *Walden, or, Life in the Woods* (New York: Signet, 1960), chapter 18.

16. Sharon Daloz Parks, *Big Questions, Worthy Dreams* (San Francisco: Jossey-Bass, 2000), 146.

17. Daniel Levinson, *The Seasons of a Man's Life* (New York: Ballantine Books, 1986). See also his later book, *The Seasons of a Woman's Life* (New York: Ballantine Books, 1997).

18. James W. Fowler, *Becoming Adult, Becoming Christian: Adult Development and Christian Faith* (San Francisco: Jossey-Bass, 2000), 25–26.

19. Daloz Parks, *Big Questions, Worthy Dreams,* 148.

20. Ibid., 152 (emphasis mine).

21. The phrase "prophetic imagination" comes from Walter Brueggemann, *The Prophetic Imagination* (1978; Minneapolis, MN: Fortress Press, 2001).

22. Marcus Borg, *The God We Never Knew: Beyond Dogmatic Religion to a More Authentic Contemporary Faith* (San Francisco, CA: HarperSanFrancisco, 1997). Borg borrows the phrase "Dream of God" from the title of a book by Verna Dozier, *The Dream of God: A Call to Return* (Boston, MA: Cowley, 1991).

23. Borg, *The God We Never Knew*, 133.

24. Ibid., 134.

25. Ibid., 141.

26. Luke 4:18.

27. Daloz Parks, *Big Questions, Worthy Dreams,* 148.

28. For interesting qualitative research on people of vision and commitment, see *Common Fire: Leading Lives of Commitment in a Complex World,* by L. A. Parks Daloz, C. H. Kean, J. P. Kean, and S. Daloz Parks (Boston, MA: Beacon Press, 1996), 148.

29. See especially Brueggemann's chapter "Prophetic Criticizing and the Embrace of Pathos," in *The Prophetic Imagination,* 39-57.

30. Bob Herbert, "The Agony of War," *The New York Times,* April 25, 2005.

31. Brueggemann, *The Prophetic Imagination,* 45.

32. Langston Hughes, "Dream Deferred (Harlem)," in *101 Great American Poems* (Mineola, NY: Dover Publications, 1998), 75.

33. John G. Neihardt, *Black Elk Speaks: Being the Life Story of a Holy Man of the Oglala Sioux* (Lincoln, NE: University of Nebraska Press, 1932), 270.

34. Jon Sobrino, *The Principle of Mercy: Taking the Crucified People from the Cross* (Maryknoll, NY: Orbis Books, 1994), 4-5.

35. Ibid., 5.

36. William F. Lynch, *Images of Hope: Imagination as Healer of the Hopeless* (New York: Mentor-Omega Books, 1965), 24.

37. Daniel Hartnett, S.J., "The Heuristics of Justice," *Proceedings of the 65th Annual Meeting of the Jesuit Philosophical Association* (2004), 15.

38. Mark 10:17–27.

7. SUFFERING

1. Leon Bloy, *Pilgrim of the Absolute*, ed. Raissa Maritain (New York: Pantheon, 1947), 349.

2. The character "Shug" in Alice Walker's novel *The Color Purple* (New York: Washington Square Press, 1982), 177.

3. Psalm 34:18.

4. M. Scott Peck, *The Road Less Traveled: A New Psychology of Love, Traditional Values, and Spiritual* Growth (New York: Touchstone/Simon & Schuster, 1978), 15.

5. Johann Wolfgang Von Goethe, "The Holy Longing," trans. Robert Bly, in *The Rag and Bone Shop of the Heart,* ed. Robert Bly, Michael Meade, and James Hillman (New York: Harper Perennial, 1993), 382.

6. C. G. Jung, *Collected Works of C. G. Jung,* Bollingen Series, No. 20, 2nd ed., trans. R. F. C. Hull (Princeton, NJ: Princeton University Press, 1973), Vol. 2, *Psychology and Religion: East and West,* 75.

7. Fyodor Dostoyevsky, *The Brothers Karamazov* (New York: Penguin Classics, 1993).

8. Rainer Maria Rilke, *Rilke on Love and Other Difficulties,* trans. John J. L. Mood (New York: W. W. Norton & Company, 1975), 31.

9. Abraham Maslow, *Toward a Psychology of Being* (New York: Von Nostrand Reinhold Company, 1962), 3–4.

10. James Hillman, *Insearch: Psychology and Religion* (1967; Woodstock, CT: Spring Publications, 1994), 55–56.

11. Jung, *Collected Works of C. G. Jung,* Vol. 10, *Civilization in Transition,* 170.

12. John A. Sanford, *Healing and Wholeness* (Mahwah, NJ: Paulist Press, 1977), 105.

13. Hillman, *Insearch,* 55–56.

14. Henri J. M. Nouwen, *The Wounded Healer: Ministry in Contemporary Society* (New York: Image Books, 1979).

15. Mircea Eliade has written the classic text on shamanism: *Shamanism: Archaic Techniques of Ecstasy* (Princeton, NJ: Princeton University Press, 1972).

16. See the chapter titled "The Great Vision," in John G. Neihardt, *Black Elk Speaks: Being the Life Story of a Holy Man of the Oglala Sioux* (Lincoln, NE: University of Nebraska Press, 1932), 20-47.

17. *Black Elk Speaks,* 49.

18. David Kinsley, *Health, Healing, and Religion: A Cross-Cultural Perspective* (Upper Saddle River, NJ: Prentice Hall, 1996), 16.

19. Dorcas is quoted in John Sanford's excellent chapter on "The Ecstatic Healer," in his book *Healing and Wholeness* (New York: Paulist Press, 1977), 67–68.

20. The stories of Jesus in the wilderness are found in Mark 1:12-13, Luke 4:1–13, and Matthew 4:1–11.

21. See Luke 4:16–30 and the original verses from Isaiah 61:1–2.

22. Isaiah 53:1–5.

23. Sanford, *Healing and Wholeness,* 81–82.

24. Dianna Ortiz (with Patricia Davis), *The Blindfold's Eyes: My Journey from Torture to Truth* (Maryknoll, NY: Orbis Books, 2002).

25. "Zero Tolerance for Torture: An Interview with Sister Dianna Ortiz, O.S.U.," *U.S. Catholic* 69, no. 1 (January 2004): 18-22.

26. Richard Stevenson, "Of the Many Deaths in Iraq, One Mother's Loss Becomes a Problem for the President," *The New York Times,* August 8, 2005.

27. Walter Brueggemann, *The Prophetic Imagination* (1978; Minneapolis, MN: Fortress Press, 2001)*,* 46.

28. John A. Sanford, *The Man Who Wrestled with God: Light from the Old Testament on the Psychology of Individuation* (Mahwah, NJ: Paulist Press, 1974), 22–23.

29. Victor Frankl, *Man's Search for Meaning* (1946; New York: Washington Square Press, 1984), 86.

30. Genesis 32:24–30.

31. Robert Ellsberg, *The Saints' Guide to Happiness* (New York: North Point Press, 2003), 121.

32. William James, *The Varieties of Religious Experience* (1902; New York: Simon & Schuster, 1997), 393.

33. Frankl, *Man's Search for Meaning*, 56–57.

34. Ibid., 57.

35. Ibid., 58. "Love is as strong as death" is a line from the Song of Songs.

36. Hebrews 4:15.

37. Hebrews 4:16.

38. *Mohandas Gandhi: Essential Writings*, ed. John Dear (Maryknoll, NY: Orbis Books, 2002), 75.

39. Matthew 5:7.

40. Jon Sobrino, *The Principle of Mercy: Taking the Crucified People from the Cross* (Maryknoll, NY: Orbis Books, 1994), 10.

41. Luke 23:33–34.

42. Brueggemann, *The Prophetic Imagination*, 96.

43. Flannery O'Connor, quoted in Ellsberg, *The Saints' Guide to Happiness,* 120.

8. CONSCIENCE

1. Russell B. Connors Jr. and Patrick T. McCormick, *Character, Choices, and Community: The Three Faces of Christian Ethics* (Mahwah, NJ: Paulist Press, 1998), 138.

2. *Morality of the Heart: A Psychology of the Christian Moral Life* is the title of a book by Charles A. Shelton (New York: Crossroad, 1997).

3. Enda McDonagh, "The Structure and Basis of Moral Experience," in *Introduction to Christian Ethics: A Reader*, ed. Ronald P. Hamel and Kenneth R. Himes (Mahwah, NJ: Paulist Press, 1989), 106–19.

4. A beautiful version of this song by the group Sweet Honey in the Rock can be heard on the CD "Feel Something Drawing Me On" (Flying Fish Records, 1992). Original words and music by Rev. W. Herbert Brewster.

5. Russell B. Connors and Patrick T. McCormick provide a review of biblical references to heart and conscience in *Character, Choices, and Community*.

6. Psalm 51:6.

7. Psalm 95:7-8.

8. Job 27:6.

9. Jeremiah 31:33.

10. Connors and McCormick, *Character, Choices, and Community,* 119.

11. Vatican Council II, *Gaudium et Spes,* Pastoral Constitution on the Church in the Modern World, 1965, 16. Adapted for inclusive language.

12. Richard M. Gula, *Moral Discernment* (Mahwah, NJ: Paulist Press, 1997).

13. Sigmund Freud, "The Ego and the Id," *The Standard Edition of the Complete Psychological Works of Sigmund Freud*, ed. J. Strachey, vol. 19 (1923; London: Hogarth Press, 1961), 53.

14. James Hillman, *Insearch: Psychology and Religion* (1967; Woodstock, CT: Spring Publications, 1994), 87. Hillman is referring to an essay on conscience in volume 10 of Jung's *Collected Works.*

15. Robert W. Firestone, *Voice Therapy: A Psychotherapeutic Approach to Self-Destructive Behavior* (New York: Human Sciences Press, 1988). Some of the material on guilt in this section is adapted from my chapter "Psychological Dimensions of the Discernment of Vocation," in *Re-Visiting the Idea of Vocation: Theological Explorations*, ed. John Haughey (Washington, DC: Catholic University of America Press, 2003).

16. Irving D. Yalom, *Existential Psychotherapy* (New York: Basic Books, 1980), 277 (emphasis mine).

17. Ibid., 281 (emphasis mine).

18. John A. Sanford, *Between People* (Mahwah, NJ: Paulist Press, 1982).

19. Ibid., 64.

20. See *The Spiritual Exercises of St. Ignatius Loyola: A Translation and Commentary,* by George Ganss, S.J. (Chicago, IL: Loyola University Press, 1992), Ex. 315.

21. Ibid., Ex. 314.

22. See the discussion of listening and obedience by Henri Nouwen, Donald McNeill, and Douglas Morrison in *Compassion: A Reflection on the Christian Life* (New York: Image Books/Doubleday, 1983), 36.

23. C.G. Jung, *The Development of Personality* (New York: Bollingen Foundation, 1954), 173.

24. Dag Hammarskjold, *Markings* (New York: Alfred A. Knopf, 1965), 205.

25. See Shelton's reflections on heart and conscience in *Morality of the Heart,* 65.

26. Richard M. Gula, "The Moral Conscience," in *Conscience: Readings in Moral Theology, No. 14*, ed. Charles E. Curran (Mahwah, NJ: Paulist Press, 2004), 61.

27. From Notebook #35, quoted in Mark Twain, *The Adventures of Huckleberry Finn* (Berkeley, CA: University of California Press, 2003).

28. Some of the passages that are most revealing of Huck's inner conflict are found in chapters 16 and 30.

29. Mark Twain, *The Adventures of Huckleberry Finn* (1884; New York: Puffin Books, 2003), 281.

30. Ibid., 282.

31. Ibid., 283.

32. Ibid., 283.

33. Jonathan Bennett, "The Conscience of Huckleberry Finn," *Philosophy* 49 (1974): 126.

34. Azar Nafisi, "The Mysterious Connections That Link Us Together," from the National Public Radio "This I Believe" series, broadcast July 18, 2005 (print version found on www.npr.org). Nafisi is the author of *Reading Lolita in Tehran.*

9. SOCIAL CONSCIENCE

1. Jon Sobrino, *The Principle of Mercy: Taking the Crucified People from the Cross* (Maryknoll, NY: Orbis Books, 1994), 1.

2. See Sobrino's chapter "Human Rights and Oppressed Peoples: Historical-Theological Reflections," in *Truth and Memory: The Church and Human Rights in El Salvador and Guatemala,* ed. M. A. Hayes and D. Tombs (London, Gracewing, 2001), 134–58.

3. Luke 4:18.

4. From the "Magnificat" of Mary, the mother of Jesus, Luke 1:52–53.

5. Quote from the documents of the 1979 Puebla conference in Peter Henriot, *Opting for the Poor: The Challenge for North Americans* (Washington, DC: Center of Concern, 1990), 21–22.

6. Leonardo Boff, *Faith on the Edge: Religion and Marginalized Existence* (San Francisco: Harper and Row, 1989), 23.

7. Sobrino, *The Principle of Mercy,* 1.

8. Daniel Hartnett, "Remembering the Poor: An Interview with Gustavo Gutierrez," *America* (February 3, 2003): 12–16.

9. From the song "Guantanamera." Original verses by Jose Marti. Lyrics and music by Jose Fernandez Diaz. Arranged and adapted by Julian Orbon, Hector Angulo, and Pete Seeger (Fall River Music, 1965).

10. Arthur Simon, *How Much Is Enough?* (Grand Rapids, MI: Baker Books, 2003), 129–30.

11. Neil Altman, *The Analyst in the Inner City: Race, Class, and Culture through a Psychoanalytic Lens* (Hillsdale, NJ: The Analytic Press, 1995), 1.

12. Oscar Romero, quoted in *The Violence of Love,* comp. and ed. James R. Brockman (1988; Maryknoll, NY: Orbis Books, 2004), 191–92.

13. The Ita Ford quotation is found in Ana Carrigan, *Salvador Witness: The Life and Calling of Jean Donovan* (Maryknoll, NY: Orbis Books, 2005), 200.

14. John 15:13.

15. Mark 10:17, 21.

16. William Butler Yeats, "The Second Coming," *The Collected Poems of W. B. Yeats,* ed. Richard J. Finneran (1921; New York: Collier Books, 1989), 187.

17. James Carroll, *Crusade: Chronicles of an Unjust War* (New York: Metropolitan Books, 2004), 2.

18. Cornel West, *Democracy Matters: Winning the Fight against Imperialism* (New York: Penguin, 2004), 12.

19. Bob Herbert, "America, a Symbol of…," *The New York Times,* May 30, 2005.

20. Dr. Martin Luther King Jr., sermon at Ebenezer Baptist Church, Atlanta, Georgia, April 30, 1967.

21. Robert Jay Lifton, *Superpower Syndrome: America's Apocalyptic Confrontation with the World* (New York: Thunder's Mouth Press, 2003).

22. For documentation of the widespread, systemic nature of the torture problem, see Mark Danner, *Torture and Truth: America, Abu Ghraib, and the War on Terror* (New York: New York Review Books, 2004).

23. "Torture Survivors Relive the Horrors," *Chicago Tribune,* May 14, 2004.

24. "Only a Few Spoke Up on Abuse as Many Soldiers Stayed Silent," *The New York Times,* May 22, 2004.

25. James Carroll, "Why Americans Back the War," *Boston Globe,* September 21, 2004.

26. From Dr. Martin Luther King Jr.'s "Beyond Vietnam" speech, delivered at Riverside Church, New York City, April 4, 1967.

27. 1 John 3:18.

28. James 2:14–17.

29. *Speak Truth to Power: Human Rights Defenders Who Are Changing Our World*, ed. Kerry Kennedy Cuomo (New York: Crown Books, 2000).

30. Excerpt from Dr. Martin Luther King Jr.'s "Beyond Vietnam" speech.

31. Story quoted in Dennis Linn, Sheila Fabricant Linn, and Matthew Linn, *Healing the Purpose of Your Life* (Mahwah, NJ: Paulist Press, 1999), 59–60.

10. CONCLUSION

1. Thomas Wolsey, in Shakespeare's *The Life of King Henry the Eighth,* Act III, scene ii.

2. H. Reinhold Niebuhr, "The Ego-Alter Dialectic and the Conscience," *Journal of Philosophy* 42 (1945): 352–59.

3. According to Saint Paul, "the fruit of the Spirit is love, joy, peace, patience, kindness, generosity, faithfulness, gentleness and self-control" (Galatians 5:22–23).

4. Daniel Berrigan, *Testimony: The Word Made Fresh* (Maryknoll, NY: Orbis Books, 2004), 175.

5. William Sloane Coffin, *Passion for the Possible: A Message to U.S. Churches,* 2nd ed. (Louisville, KY: Westminster/John Knox Press, 2004), 77.

6. Henri Nouwen, Donald McNeill, and Douglas Morrison, *Compassion: A Reflection on the Christian Life* (New York: Image Books/Doubleday, 1983), 27. Also see Dean Brackley's thoughtful reflections on downward mobility in *The Call to Discernment in Troubled Times* (New York: Crossroad, 2004).

7. *The Spiritual Exercises of St. Ignatius Loyola: A Translation and Commentary,* by George Ganss, S.J. (Chicago, IL: Loyola University Press, 1992), Ex. 167, 72–73. See also the commentary by Ganss on loving humility, 173–76.

8. Frederick Buechner, *The Hungering Dark* (San Francisco: Harper & Row, 1985), 29.

9. *My Life for the Poor: Mother Teresa of Calcutta,* ed. Jose Luis Gonzalez-Balado and Janet N. Playfoot (1985; New York: Ballantine Books, 1987), 7–8.

10. John A. Sanford, *Healing and Wholeness* (Mahwah, NJ: Paulist Press, 1977), 15.

11. Ibid.

12. Radio broadcast of interview with Dr. Cornel West on the Tavis Smiley Show, National Public Radio, November 17, 2004.

13. Paraphrase of Mark 8:36 (KJV).

14. Barbara Ehrenreich, *Fear of Falling: The Inner Life of the Middle Class* (1989; New York: Harper Perennial, 1990), 250.

15. This is the actual title of a popular self-help book by Marsha Sinetar (New York: Dell, 1987).

16. Victor Frankl, *Man's Search for Meaning* (1946; New York: Washington Square Press, 1984), 16–17.

17. Buechner, *The Hungering Dark*, 29-30.

18. C. G. Jung, *Memories, Dreams, and Reflections* (New York: Vintage Books, 1965), 297.

19. Johann Wolfgang Von Goethe, "Until One Is Committed," in *The Rag and Bone Shop of the Heart,* ed. R. Bly, J. Hillman, and M. Meade (New York: HarperCollins, 1992), 235.

20. *Field of Dreams* (Universal City, CA: Universal Studios, 1989). Movie based on the book *Shoeless Joe* by W. P. Kinsella.

21. 1 Corinthians 1:26–28.

22. Henry David Thoreau, *Walden, or, Life in the Woods* (New York: Signet, 1960), 66.

23. Robert Ellsberg, *The Saints' Guide to Happiness* (New York: North Point Press, 2003), 153.

24. From Rev. Martin Luther King Jr.'s speech at the Great March on Detroit, June 23, 1963.

25. Frankl, *Man's Search for Meaning*, 37. I have taken the liberty of using non-sexist language in the quote.

26. The "Last Judgment" passage is found in Matthew 25:31–46.

27. Rev. Martin Luther King Jr., "The Drum Major Instinct," Detroit, February 4, 1968.

28. Saying attributed to Henry David Thoreau. A similar, well-known quote, "The mass of men lead lives of quiet desperation," is found in *Walden,* 10.

29. The title poem of a collection of poetry by Jeffrey Harrison, *The Singing Underneath* (New York: E. P. Dutton, 1988).

30. From the song "Guantanamera." Original verses by Jose Marti. Lyrics and music by Jose Fernandez Diaz. Arranged and adapted by Julian Orbon, Hector Angulo, and Pete Seeger (Fall River Music, 1965).

31. David Lonsdale, *Listening to the Music of the Spirit: The Art of Discernment* (Notre Dame, IN: Ave Maria Press, 1992).

32. Sometimes known as "The Quaker Hymn," "How Can I Keep from Singing?" was written around the year 1850 by Ann Warner, who lived in New York State's Hudson Valley.

33. Gustavo Gutiérrez, *We Drink from Our Own Wells* (1984; Maryknoll, NY: Orbis Books, 2003).

34. "Redemption Song" can be heard on *Bob Marley: Songs of Freedom* (Island Records, 1999).

35. Etty Hillesum, *An Interrupted Life and Letters from Westerbork* (New York: Henry Holt and Company, 1996), 360.

36. Ibid., 73–74.

INDEX